Cooking Light

Low Calorie Cooking the Paleo and Grain Free Way

Rhonda Price

Table of Contents

Cooking Light: Introduction

The Paleo Diet, though an ancient diet, has regained popularity recently due to the discovery of the condition of our ancient Stone Age ancestors. This diet is also called The Stone Age Diet, The Caveman Diet or the Hunter-Gatherer Diet. The diet is based on the observation of how our Stone Age ancestors ate and the state of their health as evidence through their discovered bones. These people were avid hunters, hunting, killing, and eating mostly meat. They also ate wild plants, and did not tend to "garden" much, as we know it today. They did not eat grains or legumes, because they did not know about those types of plants.

The Paleo Diet as we know it takes the concept of our Stone Age ancestors and adapted the diet to the foods we have available to us today. Basically, it consists of all meats from pasture animals and fish as well as vegetables, fruit, roots, nuts and fungus (mushrooms). The diet strictly excludes dairy, refined sugars and flours, grains, potatoes, and legumes.

The Paleo Diet made a resurgence in the 1970's when

Walter L. Voegtlin, a gastroenterologist, researched the concept of the diet of our ancestors. He believed that humans originally ate the Paleo Diet and that through the centuries man has had to adapt to all the diet changes, even though genetics has not changed that much. The result of all the adaptations is diseases and ill health conditions that occur because our body is not meant to eat the way most do today. He believed that by resorting back to the diet of the first people we could realign our genetics to the healthy state we started with in the first place.

The Stone Age people were a healthy lot; living long lives free of cardiovascular and weight issues. Because we know that diet does play a major role in the state of our health, we can trace their longevity and health to their diet and nutrition.

Opponents of the Paleo Diet claim it to be just a "fad" diet that does not hold much truth to it being a nutritious diet. These people believe that health issues do not stem solely from diet but from other influences, such as exposure to social diseases, genetic disposition to live a shorter life, and in eating too little or too much calories and not necessarily the composition of the food.

The argument now for and against the Paleo Diet is that

the foods we consume today are not like the foods consumed in the Stone Age. We eat meats that are higher in fat, vegetables, fruits that have been altered, and the addition of processed foods and grains. If we could truly eat as our Stone Age ancestors, we would eat ultra lean meats and wild plants that grew naturally in nature without any help or alteration by man.

Proponents claim the diet offers a version of the popular "low carb" diet because of the high protein and the absence of grains. The Paleo Diet does have high nutritional value if you consider the nutrients found in raw vegetables, especially green leafy vegetables and root vegetables, which are high in anti-oxidants. By eating the Paleo Diet, you are consuming more of this and not consuming processed foods, which have no nutritional value. In fact, most all of the foods on the Paleo Diet have a good amount of nutrients, which helps the body to build a strong immune system.

Learning what foods are on the Paleo Diet will help in making the right choices when going grocery shopping and when eating out too. Since the Paleo Diet is primarily a meat eating diet this is the list of meats: anchovy, bear, beef, bison, chicken, clams, cod, crab, deer, duck, elk, flatfish, goat, goose, grouper, herring, horse, lamb, lobster, mackerel, moose, mussels, oysters, pheasant, pork, quail, rabbit, salmon, scallops, sheep, shrimp, tilapia, trout, tuna, turkey, veal, walleye, wild boar, wild turkey, and woodcock.

Other proteins included are: eggs of all kinds including chicken, duck, god and quail. Nuts such as almonds, brazil nuts, cashews, chestnuts, hazelnuts, macadamia nuts, pecans, pine nuts, pistachios, pumpkin seeds, sesame seeds, sunflower seeds, and walnuts. Mushrooms are protein and of these the Paleo Diet include: button mushroom, chanterelle, crimini, oyster mushroom, porcini, portabella, and shiitake.

The fats included on the Paleo Diet are: avocados, avocado oil, butter, coconut (all parts), duck fat, ghee, lamb fat, lard, macadamia oil, nut butters, olive oil, sardines, tallow, veal fat, and walnut oil.

The vegetables on the Paleo Diet include: acorn squash, arugula, artichokes, asparagus, beets and beet top, bell peppers, bok choy, broccoli, Brussels sprouts, butternut squash, cabbage, carrots, cassava, cauliflower, celery, chicory, collard green, cucumber, dandelion, eggplants, endive, green onions, Jerusalem artichokes, kale, kohlrabi, leeks, lettuce, mustard greens, okra, onions, parsnips, radicchio, radish, rapini, rutabaga, seaweed, spinach, spaghetti squash, sweet potatoes, Swiss chard, tomatoes, turnip greens and turnips, watercress, yams, and yellow squash.

The Paleo Diet fruits list includes: apples, apricot, bananas, blackberries, blueberries, cantaloupe, cherries, cranberries, dates, figs, grapefruit, grapes, honeydew melon, kiwi, lemon, lime, lychee, mango, nectarines, oranges, papaya, passion fruit, peaches, pears, persimmon, pineapple, plums, pomegranates, strawberries, tangerine, and water melon.

The Paleo Diet includes herbs and spices too: bay leaves, basil, black pepper, cayenne pepper, chives, cinnamon, cloves, coriander, cumin, dill, fennel seeds, garlic, ginger, hot peppers, lavender, mint, mustard seeds, nutmeg, onions, oregano, paprika, parsley, rosemary, sage, star anise, tarragon, thyme, turmeric, and vanilla.

The next sections cover the recipes for the Paleo Diet including entrees, side dishes, soups, snacks, breakfast, and desserts. Each of the recipes are original, however many are inspired by other recipes found in books, on websites and through sharing. Recipes have been around since the beginning of time, so it is likely you may find some similar to what you see elsewhere. The recipes in this book are all considered "light" eating and staying in compliance with the recommendations of the

Paleo Diet. Feel free to modify and change recipes as you see fit.

Section 1: Paleo Cookbook

What is the Paleo Diet?

Also known as the caveman diet and the Stone Age diet, the Paleo diet is a diet which is low in sugar, low in sodium, largely dairy free and relatively high in protein. It's a diet based on the foods which would have been available to our pre-agrarian Neolithic ancestors. The Paleo diet isn't a carb-free or low carb diet, per se, but it is free of grains, with carbohydrates coming from fresh vegetables and fruits rather than grains.

This is also a diet which steers clear of processed foods, at least for the most part – and any processed foods included in the diet are as minimally changed from their natural state as possible. While you obviously don't have to hunt or gather your own ingredients (and to be honest, the diet does include many vegetables which weren't really developed until we started to settle down in agrarian communities), the idea is to avoid the modern processed foods which can wreak havoc on your health.

Better health is really the main goal of the diet and while

it isn't actually geared towards weight loss, many people who adopt the Paleo diet do indeed experience weight loss, especially when combined with regular exercise. It really comes down to common sense for the most part. The Paleo diet is rich in natural, fresh foods – in short, the kind of food which we know that we should be eating in the first place.

Fresh produce, meat and nuts are the major players in these Paleo diet recipes. Following this diet will require a little bit of adjustment on your part and a little more time in the kitchen, at least until you get the hang of things – but once you start enjoying the health benefits of the Paleo diet, we think you'll agree it's a change well worth making. From main dishes to salads, soups to desserts and breakfast and brunch, these recipes cover all of the basics – so without further ado, let's get cooking, Paleo style!

Entrees

Roasted Turkey with Balsamic Glaze and Apples

Number of servings: 8 – 10

Ingredients:

1 medium-sized turkey (10 – 15 lbs), thawed
10 Granny Smith apples, cored and halved (peeling is optional)
4 sprigs of rosemary
4 cloves of garlic, crushed
½ cup balsamic vinegar
½ cup olive oil
1 tbsp salt
black pepper, to taste

Preparation:

Preheat your oven to 325 F. Remove the gizzards from the turkey, then rinse the turkey well and pat dry with paper towels. Truss up the legs with string. Place the rosemary sprigs and 2 apple halves inside of the bird and place the turkey, breast up, in a large roasting pan. Surround the turkey with apple halves and drizzle with the balsamic vinegar and olive oil. Sprinkle the turkey with the salt and black pepper.

Place the roasting pan on the lowest rack in your oven and roast for 15 minutes per pound – a 15 pound turkey will take just a little under 4 hours. Check the turkey periodically after it's been roasting for about 2 hours; if the skin starts to brown earlier than you'd like, cover the roasting pan with foil to slow down browning. Test the turkey with a meat thermometer placed deep into the flesh of the thigh. When the thermometer reads 175 F, the turkey is done and is safe to eat. Remove the roasting pan from the oven and allow the turkey to rest for at least 20 minutes. Carve and serve.

Gluten Free Chicken Piccata

Number of servings: 4

Ingredients:

4 chicken breast halves
1 cup chicken or vegetable stock
½ cup of almond flour
½ cup of olive oil
¼ cup of capers
¼ cup of Italian parsley, chopped
¼ cup of lemon juice (about 2 lemons worth of juice)
½ tsp salt
½ tsp Italian seasoning
black pepper, to taste

Preparation:

Butterfly the chicken breast halves; cut them into two pieces after butterflying if they're especially large. Place the chicken between two pieces of parchment paper or wax paper and using a cast iron skillet or mallet, pound the chicken breasts until they're about ¼" thick.
After flattening the chicken breasts, mix the almond flour, Italian seasoning and salt in a bowl; pour the flour

mixture on a plate. Dip the chicken breast pieces in water and dredge in the almond flour mixture to coat.

Heat half of the olive oil in a large skillet over medium-high heat. Brown the chicken pieces well on both sides (this will take about 3 minutes per side); you will probably need to do this in two batches. Place the browned chicken breasts on a plate in a warm oven to stay warm while you make the sauce.

Deglaze the skillet with the chicken or vegetable stock and add the capers and lemon juice, then bring to a simmer over medium-high heat until reduced by half. Whisk in the remaining olive oil to incorporate. Place the chicken on individual serving plates, season to taste with black pepper and top with the sauce and chopped parsley before serving.

Chicken with Cherries and Kale

Number of servings: 4

Ingredients:

1 ½ lbs chicken breast, boneless and skinless
10 ounces of fresh or frozen cherries
1 bunch of kale, stems removed and sliced into thin ribbons
4 tbsp of olive oil
2 tbsp of balsamic vinegar
2 tbsp of minced shallots
1 tbsp of Dijon mustard
salt and black pepper, to taste

Preparation:

Rinse the chicken breasts, pat dry and place between 2 sheets of parchment paper or waxed paper. Pound the chicken breasts until they're about 1/4" thick with a cast iron skillet or a mallet; while you're doing this, start heating half of the olive oil in a large skillet over medium heat. Once the oil is hot, add the minced shallots and sauté until fragrant, about one minute. Add the cherries and cook for another 2 – 3 minutes, or until the cherries soften. Add the mustard, balsamic vinegar and kale. Cook, covered, until the kale is wilted, stirring occasionally, about 5 minutes.

In another skillet, heat the other half of the oil over medium high heat. Once the oil is hot, place the chicken breasts in the pan. Sprinkle with a little salt and pepper and cook for about 5 minutes per side, or until the chicken is cooked through and nicely browned. Transfer the chicken to the other skillet with the kale and cherries and cook over low heat for another few minutes to allow the chicken to take on some of the flavor of the sauce. Serve hot, topped with the cherry sauce.

Chipotle - Lime Salmon

Number of servings: 4

Ingredients:

4 salmon filets, about 4 ounces each
2 limes, halved
2 tbsp of olive oil
1 tsp chipotle powder
1 tsp salt
black pepper, to taste

Preparation:

Start by preheating your oven to 500 F. While the oven heats, rinse the salmon, pat dry with paper towels and place on a lightly oiled baking sheet. Brush each salmon filet with a little olive oil, squeeze half a lime over each filet and sprinkle with a little salt and ¼ of the chipotle powder. Top each filet with a lime half. Place the baking sheet in the oven and reduce the heat to 300 F. Bake for 8 – 10 minutes or to your desired level of doneness.

Cobb Salad

Number of servings: 4

Ingredients:

1 small chicken breast (about ½ lb), cooked and chilled
1 cup of cherry tomatoes, halved
1 avocado, peeled, seeded and diced
4 eggs, hard boiled, cooled, peeled and quartered
8 pieces of turkey, cooked until crisp and crumbled into small pieces
6 large leaves of romaine lettuce, sliced into thin ribbons
ranch dressing and black pepper, to taste

Preparation:

Cut the chicken breast into ½" pieces. Divide the lettuce among 4 individual plates or salad bowls and top with the chicken, avocado, cherry tomatoes and crumbled turkey. Place egg wedges on the sides of the dish, add a generous sprinkle of black pepper and serve with ranch dressing on the side.

Hot Dogs, Paleo Style

Number of servings: 4

Ingredients:

4 hot dogs
4 romaine lettuce leaves

Preparation:

Cook the hot dogs any way that you prefer; you can boil them, grill them or fry them up in a hot skillet with a little bit of olive or coconut oil. Place each cooked hot dog on a piece of romaine lettuce and then top with mustard, sauerkraut, chopped onions or any other condiments you like. Serve at once.

Green Chili Turkey Burgers

Number of servings: 4 - 6

Ingredients:

1 lb ground turkey
8 oz diced canned green chilies
1 cup of finely chopped cilantro
1 small red onion, diced small
2 tsp of cumin
1 tsp salt
1 tsp of chili powder

Preparation:

Mix all of the ingredients for your green chili turkey burgers in a bowl; use your hands as you would when mixing meatloaf in order to ensure that the ingredients are evenly distributed throughout. Shape the turkey mixture into burgers (of whatever size you'd like) and grill or pan-fry them until they're completely cooked through and well browned on the outside. Serve the burgers on lettuce leaves with the condiments and toppings of your choice.

Shepherd's Pie, Paleo Style

Number of servings: 8

Ingredients:

2 large heads of cauliflower, chopped and steamed until
very soft
1 lb ground beef (preferably grass fed organic beef)
1 lb turkey, cut into 2" long pieces
2 cups of diced celery
2 cups of diced carrots
1 large onion, diced
4 cloves of garlic, minced
1 cup chicken or vegetable stock
2 tbsp of olive oil
1 tsp smoked paprika
1 tsp thyme
salt and black pepper, to taste

Preparation:

Heat the olive oil in a large skillet over medium heat.
Once the oil is hot, add the onion and garlic and sauté
until soft, about 5 minutes. Add the bacon (or
alternative) to the pan and cook for another 7 – 10

minutes until the turkey is done. Add the celery and carrots and cook until soft, about 7 minutes. Add the ground beef and sauté, stirring regularly for about 5 minutes or until the beef is browned. Season the mixture with the smoked paprika, salt and black pepper, then add the chicken or vegetable stock and cook the mixture down until only about 1/3 of the liquid remains in the skillet.

While the stock is cooking down, preheat your oven to 350 F and puree the cauliflower in a blender or food processor with a little olive oil until smooth. Season with a little salt and black pepper. Remove the beef mixture from heat and pour into a large (9" x 13") baking dish. Top the beef with the pureed cauliflower. Transfer the baking dish to your oven and bake, uncovered, for about 30 minutes or until the cauliflower is slightly browned. Remove from the oven, allow to rest for 5 minutes, slice and serve.

Salmon with Red Pepper Sauce and Mushrooms

Number of servings:

Ingredients:

4 salmon filets, about 6 ounces each
2 large red bell peppers, roughly chopped
2/3 cup of sliced shiitake mushrooms
1 small white onion, diced
3 tbsp of olive oil
juice of 1 lemon
½ tsp salt, plus more to taste
1 tbsp Italian parsley, minced
black pepper, to taste

Preparation:

Start by making a red bell pepper puree. Preheat your
oven to 350 F while you rinse and chop the peppers,
removing the pith and seeds before you chop them.
Place the chopped red peppers on a baking sheet or
dish, place in the oven and bake for 15 – 20 minutes, or
until the skins shrivel. Remove the peppers from the
oven and set aside to cool. Add the peppers, lemon juice
and ½ tsp salt to a blender or food processor and blend

until pureed. Transfer the red pepper puree to a small saucepan over low heat to keep warm until you're ready to assemble the dish.

Next, you'll prepare the mushrooms. Heat 2 tbsp of olive oil in a skillet over medium heat. Once the oil is hot, sauté the onions for 1 -2 minutes and add the mushrooms. Reduce the heat to medium-low, cover and cook for 7 – 10 minutes, or until the mushrooms are soft. Add black pepper to taste.

While the mushrooms are cooking, preheat your oven to 500 F. Rinse the salmon and pat dry, brush with the other 1 tbsp of olive oil and place on a baking sheet. Sprinkle the salmon filets with a little salt and black pepper, place in the oven on the bottom rack and reduce the heat to 300 F. Bake for about 10 minutes, or until the centers of the filets are still slightly translucent. Remove the salmon from the oven and set aside.

Spoon ¼ of the red pepper puree onto each plate, topped by a salmon filet and then a portion of the mushrooms and a sprinkling of chopped parsley. Serve immediately.

Paleo-Style Stuffed Peppers

Number of servings: 6

Ingredients:

6 bell peppers (any color)
1 lb ground turkey
8 ounces diced green chilies
1 medium onion, diced small
1 cup minced cilantro
2 tsp cumin
1 tsp salt
1 tsp chili powder
black pepper, to taste

Preparation:

Mix the ground turkey, green chilies, cilantro, onion and spices together in a bowl by hand, mixing well. Cut the tops off of the bell peppers and reserve. Blanch the peppers for about 1 minute in boiling water, then immediately place in cold water. Preheat your oven to 350 F.

Once the peppers are cooled, stuff them with the turkey

mixture and replace the tops of the peppers. Place the peppers in a baking dish and bake for 1 hour; serve hot.

Coconut Chicken Strips

Number of servings: 2

Ingredients:

2 chicken breasts, boneless and skinless
1 cup shredded coconut
½ cup coconut flour
2 eggs
a splash of coconut milk
salt and black pepper, to taste

Preparation:

Start by preheating your oven to 400 F. While the oven heats, place the chicken breasts between pieces of parchment paper or wax paper and pound flat until they reach an even thickness. Slice the flattened chicken breasts into long, 1" wide strips.

Beat together the eggs and coconut milk in a small bowl. Place the coconut flour and shredded coconut on two separate plates. Dredge the chicken strips in coconut flour, then dip in the egg mixture, then roll in shredded coconut and place on a baking sheet. Bake for 12 minutes, or until the chicken is cooked through and the outside is browned and crisp. Serve at once with the condiments of your choice.

Taco Pie

Number of servings: 4

Ingredients:

For the crust:
1 ½ cups almond flour
¼ cup butter or ghee, melted
1 tsp salt
For the filling:
1 lb ground beef (preferably grass fed organic beef)
1 small white onion, diced
1 cup chopped lettuce
1 bell pepper (any color), sliced
1 avocado, peeled, seeded and sliced
1 tbsp olive oil
1 tbsp minced cilantro
½ cup salsa, your choice, plus more for serving
salt and black pepper, to taste

Preparation:

First, make the crust for your pie. Add the almond flour, salt and butter to a large bowl and mix until it takes on a dough-like texture. Turn out the dough into a 9" pie dish and press out with your hands until it covers the dish evenly. Place in the refrigerator until you're ready to assemble the pie and preheat your oven to 350 F.

Now you're ready to prepare the filling for your taco pie. Heat the olive oil over medium-high heat in a large skillet and sauté the onions just until they turn translucent, then add the ground beef and cook, stirring regularly, until the beef is well browned. Stir in the salsa and add salt and black pepper to taste. Cook for another 1 -2 minutes to warm through and remove from heat.

Pour the beef mixture into the pie crust and bake for 35 minutes. Top with chopped lettuce, bell pepper slices, avocado slices and salsa and serve hot.

Pork Roast with Dijon Glaze

Number of servings: 4

Ingredients:

1 pork (or alternative) roast, about 3 lbs
2 tbsp cumin
2 tbsp garlic powder
2 tbsp chopped cilantro
2 tbsp smoked paprika
1 tbsp salt
1 tbsp black pepper
¼ cup olive oil
3 tbsp Dijon mustard
3 tbsp water

Preparation:

Start by preheating your oven to 425 F. While your oven is heating, place the pork (or alternative) roast in a large baking dish and score the surface of the roast with a knife. Next, mix together the spices and salt in a small bowl. Rub the roast with the spice mixture. Sprinkle the chopped cilantro on top of the roast.

Place the roast in the oven and cook for 15 minutes, then reduce the heat to 350 F and continue baking for another 15 minutes. While the roast cooks at 350 F, whisk together the olive oil, mustard and water to make the glaze.

After the roast has been cooking at 350 F for 15 minutes, remove from the oven and brush well with the glaze. Return the roast to the oven and cook for another 45 minutes; when a meat thermometer inserted into the thickest part of the roast reads 150 F, it's done. Remove from the oven and allow to rest for 5 minutes, then carve and serve.

Cabbage and Ham Stew

Number of servings: 6

Ingredients:

1 lb cooked ham (or alternative), diced
½ of a large head of cabbage (green or red), chopped
1 large onion, diced
1 bell pepper (any color), diced
2 medium carrots, diced
4 cloves of garlic, minced
6 – 8 cups vegetable stock

2 bay leaves
salt and black pepper, to taste

Preparation:

Heat the olive oil in a large saucepan over medium-high heat. Sauté the onions and garlic for 5 – 7 minutes, just until they start to turn translucent. Add the chopped cabbage, diced carrots and diced ham and cook for 5 minutes, stirring frequently.

Add the stock and bay leaves and bring to a simmer and cook, partially covered for 35 minutes. Continue cooking until most of the liquid has been evaporated. Remove from heat, remove the bay leaves, season to taste with salt and black pepper and serve.

Roast Chicken

Number of servings: 2

Ingredients:

2 chicken breasts, boneless and skinless
3 tbsp olive oil
a pinch of thyme
salt and black pepper, to taste

Preparation:

Start by preheating your oven to 375 F. Place the chicken breasts in a baking dish and drizzle with the olive oil. Sprinkle the chicken with salt, black pepper and thyme. Bake for 40 – 45 minutes, or until the juices run clear.

Fish Tacos

Number of servings: 4

Ingredients:

1 lb tilapia or other white fish filets
1 medium sized white or red onion, diced
1 medium sized tomato, diced
4 cloves of garlic, minced
1 – 2 jalapeno or Serrano peppers, diced small
2 tbsp minced cilantro
1 tbsp olive oil
juice of 2 limes
salt and black pepper, to taste
salsa, sliced avocado and romaine lettuce leaves, for
serving

Preparation:

Heat the olive oil in a large skillet over medium-high
heat. Once the oil is hot, sauté the onions and garlic for
5 minutes, stirring occasionally, or until the onions are
translucent. Add the tilapia filets and cook for 3 – 4
minutes, then flip and flake with a fork. Add the
tomatoes, cilantro, jalapeno or Serrano peppers and

lime juice. Season to taste with salt and black pepper and cook for another 4 – 5 minutes, then remove from heat. Serve the tilapia mixture on romaine lettuce leaves with avocado slices and salsa.

Beef Stroganoff

Number of servings: 4

Ingredients:

1 lb top sirloin, sliced into strips
1 medium sized yellow onion, diced
1 cup sliced mushrooms (button or crimini)
1 cup coconut milk
1 cup beef stock
¼ cup dry white wine
2 cloves of garlic, minced
4 tbsp butter, ghee or olive oil
1 tbsp chopped Italian parsley
salt and black pepper, to taste

Preparation:

Heat 2 tbsp of butter, ghee or olive oil in a large, heavy skillet over medium-high heat. Add the beef and cook for about a minute on each side to brown slightly. Transfer to a plate and set aside. Add the mushroom to the skillet and cook just until browned slightly. Transfer to a plate and set aside. Next, add the onions and garlic to the skillet and cook for just a minute, then deglaze the skillet with the white wine. Cook until the alcohol burns off and add the beef broth and coconut milk. Whisk to combine the ingredients into a creamy sauce. Return the mushrooms and beef strips to the skillet and simmer for 5 minutes, taking care not to overcook the beef. Remove from heat and serve hot over spaghetti squash, zucchini noodles or mashed cauliflower.

Shakshouka

Number of servings: 4

Ingredients:

4 cups diced tomatoes
4 large or extra large eggs
1 red bell pepper, seeded and diced
1 small onion, diced
2 cloves of garlic, minced
2 tbsp tomato paste
1 tbsp olive oil
1 tsp paprika
1 tsp cumin
salt, black pepper and crushed red pepper, to taste

Preparation:

Heat the olive oil in a large skillet (a cast iron skillet is best for this recipe) over medium heat. Once the oil is hot, add the onions and garlic and sauté, stirring occasionally, until the garlic and onion are tender and slightly browned, about 5 minutes. Add the diced red bell pepper and cook for another 5 minutes, or until the pepper is just tender. Add the tomato paste and diced tomatoes, along with the paprika, a little salt and crushed red pepper. Taste and adjust the seasonings as needed. Keep the mixture on a low simmer.

Crack the eggs over the tomato mixture, trying to space them evenly over the skillet. Cover and cook for 5 – 10 minutes, or until the eggs reach your desired level of doneness (sunny side up will be about 5 minutes, but closer to 10 minutes if you'd prefer them well done). Serve garnished with parsley.

Salmon with Cherry Tomatoes and Roasted Asparagus

Number of servings: 4

Ingredients:

The salmon:
4 salmon filets, 4 -6 ounces each
2 cloves of garlic, minced
juice and zest of ½ lemon
1 tbsp olive oil
½ tsp salt
½ tsp paprika
black pepper, to taste
The asparagus:
1 bunch asparagus, washed and trimmed
1 tbsp olive oil
a splash of lemon juice
salt and black pepper, to taste
The cherry tomato salsa:
½ cup quartered cherry tomatoes
1 clove of garlic, minced
juice and zest of ½ of a lime
1 tbsp olive oil
2 tbsp fresh oregano, chopped
a pinch of salt

black pepper, to taste

Preparation:

Preheat your oven to 400 F. While the oven heats, mix together the olive oil, lemon juice and zest, minced garlic and a little salt and pepper. Place the salmon and marinade in a container with a tightly-fitting lid, shake to coat and refrigerate for half an hour.
While the salmon is marinating, you can prepare the roasted asparagus. Place the trimmed asparagus on a baking sheet, drizzled with lemon juice, olive oil, salt and black pepper and bake for 10 – 15 minutes, turning every 5 minutes until the asparagus is cooked through and nicely browned. Remove from the oven, divide among 4 individual serving plates and turn the heat up to broil.

Next, make the cherry tomato salsa. Add all of the ingredients to a small bowl and toss to combine. Refrigerate until you're ready to serve the salmon. Place the marinated salmon filets on a foil-lined baking sheet and broil for 8 minutes per inch of thickness – remove from the oven and serve over a bed of roasted asparagus, topped with a dollop of the cherry tomato salsa.

Stuffed Pork Tenderloin

Number of servings: 4

Ingredients:

1 pork (or alternative) tenderloin (about 2 lbs)
1 small onion, diced
6 sun dried tomatoes, chopped
2 artichoke hearts, chopped
1 egg
2 cloves of garlic, minced or crushed
2 tbsp olive oil or ghee
½ tsp sage
½ tsp thyme
½ tsp nutmeg
salt and black pepper, to taste

Preparation:

Heat the olive oil in a skillet over medium-high heat and sauté the onion, garlic, sun dried tomatoes and artichoke hearts. Sauté for 3 – 5 minutes, stirring regularly until the onions are translucent and the artichokes and sun dried tomatoes become tender. Remove from heat and set aside.

Place the tenderloin in a large baking dish and drizzle with a little olive oil, then sprinkle with salt and pepper. Cut the tenderloin lengthwise down the center to create a seam that allows you to stuff it and set aside until the stuffing is ready.

Preheat your oven to 450 F while you prepare the stuffing. Whisk an egg into the ingredients in the skillet – make sure that they're cooled to room temperature before you do this, since you need the egg to cook once it's inside the pork tenderloin, not before.
Place the stuffing into the seam of the pork tenderloin; get as much of the stuffing in as you can, but take care not to overstuff it to the point that you can't fold it closed. Use toothpicks to secure the tenderloin while it cooks.

Place the pork tenderloin in the oven and cook, uncovered for 30 minutes. After 30 minutes, lower the heat to 300 F and cook for another 20 minutes. Turn off the oven, but don't remove the tenderloin from the oven for another 15 minutes. Remove from the oven, remove the toothpicks, slice and serve.

Paleo Pizza

Number of servings: 4

Ingredients:

The crust:
1 cup almond meal
½ cup coconut flour
4 eggs
3 tbsp olive oil
2 tsp garlic powder
1 tsp baking powder
The topping:
2 – 4 tbsp tomato sauce or pesto
8 sun dried tomatoes, chopped
3 artichoke hearts, chopped finely
4 - 8 button or crimini mushrooms, sliced
¼ to ½ cup sliced ham (or alternative)
1 tbsp coconut oil

Preparation:

Start by preheating your oven to 375 F while you make
the crust. Making the crust will take significantly longer
than the rest of the preparation, so do this first. Mix

together the dry ingredients in a large bowl, stirring well to distribute evenly. Add the wet ingredients, using a whisk to stir. Once the mixture becomes too stiff to mix with a whisk, use your hands to knead – it will form very soft dough. Oil a pizza pan and pour in the dough. Spread it to cover the entire surface as evenly as possible. Place the crust in the oven and bake for 20 minutes.

While the crust bakes, prepare your toppings. The only one which needs cooking is the mushrooms. Heat the coconut oil in a small saucepan or skillet over medium heat and sauté the mushrooms for 3 – 5 minutes or until cooked.

Once the crust has been baking for 20 minutes, remove it from the oven and spread with tomato or pesto sauce (as little or as much as you like). Add the sun dried tomatoes, chopped artichokes, mushrooms and ham. Return the pizza to the oven and cook for another 10 – 12 minutes. Remove from the oven, slice and serve.

Hearty Beef Stew

Number of servings: 4

Ingredients:

1 lb beef (use pre-cut beef stew meat or use any good cut of beef cut into ½" – 1" pieces)
4 cups beef stock
3 ½ cups diced tomatoes (canned or fresh)
2 small or 1 very large onion, diced (about 1 cup)
1 cup diced celery
1 cup diced carrots
1 – 2 potatoes, cubed
2 tbsp olive oil
1 tsp fresh rosemary, minced
1 tsp fresh thyme leaves, or more to taste
salt and black pepper, to taste

Preparation:

Add the olive oil, onions, carrots, celery and potatoes to a large saucepan or stock pot over medium-high heat. Sauté the vegetables for about 5 minutes, stirring occasionally to prevent burning. Add the beef and cook for a few minutes to brown, then add the tomatoes, herbs and beef stock, along with a little salt and black pepper.

Bring to a simmer and cook, covered, for 1 – 1 ½ hours, stirring every 20 minutes or so while it cooks. Remove the lid from the pot and cook for another 45 minutes, uncovered. If the stew is a little thicker than you like at this point, add a little beef stock or water to bring it to your desired consistency and cook for a few minutes to warm through.

Paleo Chili

Number of servings: 12 - 16

Ingredients:

5 lbs ground beef (preferably grass fed organic beef)
12 cups diced tomatoes, canned or fresh
4 cups sliced button or crimini mushrooms
12 cloves of garlic, minced
2 onions, diced
3 celery stalks, diced
3 carrots, diced
1 small bunch of Italian flat leaf parsley, chopped
3 bay leaves
3 sprigs of thyme
2 tbsp olive oil
salt and black pepper, to taste

Preparation:

Cook the ground beef over medium heat in a large, heavy skillet until browned. Remove from heat and set aside when done. Either after the beef is cooked or while it's cooking, sauté the garlic and onions in olive oil over medium heat in a stock pot or very large saucepan.

Cook for about 3 minutes, or until the garlic and onions are very fragrant. Add the carrots, mushrooms and celery and cook for 5 – 10 minutes, stirring regularly. Add the diced tomatoes and ground beef. Stir well to combine the ingredients, then add the bay leaves, chopped parsley and thyme. Reduce the heat to a low simmer and cook, uncovered for 3 – 4 hours or until the chili reaches your desired consistency, stirring occasionally. Season to taste with salt and black pepper and serve.

Spicy Scallop Salad

Number of servings: 4

Ingredients:

1 lb scallops
1 red bell pepper, seeded and cut into strips
1 avocado, peeled, seeded and diced
2 cups mixed salad greens
½ cup olive oil plus 2 tbsp olive oil for cooking
juice of 2 lemons
1 clove of garlic, minced
2 tsp black pepper
2 tsp cayenne pepper or more to taste
1 tsp Dijon mustard
1 tsp salt
2 tsp cayenne pepper
salt and black pepper, to taste

Preparation:

First, assemble the rest of the salad (other than the scallops). Combine the greens, red bell pepper strips and diced avocado in a large bowl. Toss gently to distribute the ingredients evenly.

Next, make your dressing. Add the lemon juice, mustard, salt and cayenne pepper, along with salt and black pepper to taste and whisk together. Add the olive oil a little at a time, whisking to combine.

In a large bowl, mix the salt, black pepper and cayenne with the scallops, tossing until the scallops are evenly coated. Heat the rest of the olive oil in a large, heavy skillet over medium – high heat. The oil needs to be hot before you start cooking the scallops, since the idea is to sear them; however, don't let the oil get so hot that it begins to smoke. Once the skillet is hot, add the scallops to the skillet and cook for 2 minutes per side; the scallops should be just cooked through and opaque. Add the scallops to the salad bowl, then pour the dressing over the top. Serve immediately while the scallops are still hot.

Paleo Meatloaf

Number of servings: 4

Ingredients:

1 ½ lbs lean ground beef (preferably grass fed organic beef)
1 small yellow or white onion, diced small
1 cup chopped red cabbage
4 cloves of garlic, minced
½ cup barbecue sauce
1/3 cup almond meal
1 large egg, beaten
2 tbsp coconut milk
1 tsp salt
1 tsp dry mustard
1 tsp black pepper, or more to taste
1 tsp garlic powder
1 tsp chipotle powder
1 tsp sage
1 tsp hot pepper sauce

Preparation:

Start by preheating your oven to 350 F. Combine all of

the ingredients with the exception of the ground beef and barbecue sauce in a large bowl and stir well to combine. Add the ground beef and mix well using a fork (or your hands, which is messier but also much easier to do).

Transfer the ground beef mixture into an ungreased loaf pan and pour the barbecue sauce over the meatloaf. Place the meatloaf in the oven and bake, uncovered, for 80 – 90 minutes. When a meat thermometer inserted in the middle of the meatloaf reads at least 160 F, it's done. Remove from the oven, allow it to rest for 5 minutes, then slice and serve hot.

Pork Tenderloin with Blueberries

Number of servings: 2

Ingredients:

2 pork (or lamb) tenderloins, about ¼ lb each
1 lb green beans, trimmed
1 small white or red onion, diced small
1 ½ cups blueberries, fresh or frozen and thawed
¼ cup apple cider vinegar or red wine vinegar
4 tsp olive oil
4 tsp poultry seasoning

2 tsp honey
2 tsp thyme
salt and black pepper, to taste

Preparation:

First, preheat your oven to 400 F. Rub the pork (or lamb) tenderloins with the poultry seasoning and a little salt and black pepper. Place the pork in a roasting pan and cook for 25 minutes, or until a meat thermometer inserted in the thickest part of the tenderloin reads 155 F. After the pork tenderloins have been in the oven for 15 minutes, remove the roasting pan from the oven and surround the pork with the green beans. Drizzle the green beans with half of the olive oil, stir and return to the oven quickly.

Now, heat the other half of the olive oil over medium – high heat in a small saucepan. Add the diced onion and cook for 5 minutes, until the onions start to turn translucent, stirring occasionally. Add the blueberries, honey, vinegar, thyme and salt and black pepper to taste. Cook the sauce for another 5 minutes, or until it thickens. When it's finished, remove the pork from the oven and serve with the blueberry sauce drizzled on top and green beans on the side.

Baked Salmon with Pecans and Rosemary

Number of servings: 2

Ingredients:

1 salmon filet (3/4 lb to 1 lb)
2 tbsp chopped pecans
1 tbsp rosemary leaves, minced
1 tsp salt
black pepper, to taste
coconut oil

Preparation:

Start by preheating your oven to 350 F while you prepare the ingredients. Lightly oil a baking sheet with coconut oil. Lay the salmon filet on the baking sheet, skin side down. Sprinkle the salmon with the chopped pecans, minced rosemary and a little salt and black pepper. Place the baking sheet in the oven and bake for 12 – 14 minutes, or until the salmon can be easily flaked with a fork.

Side Dishes, Soups and Snacks

Chicken Soup with Sweet Potatoes and Swiss Chard

Number of servings: 4 - 6

Ingredients:

2 lbs chicken thighs, skinless and boneless

6 cups of water

4 cups chicken stock or vegetable stock

1 bunch Swiss chard, chopped

1 large sweet potato, diced

1 bunch of green onions, trimmed and sliced thinly

1 medium sized yellow onion, diced

1 medium sized carrot, diced small

1 celery stalk, diced small

4 cloves of garlic, minced

2 jalapeno peppers, diced (you can remove the seeds for a milder flavor if you like)

juice of 1 lemon

2 tbsp olive oil

1 tsp thyme

1 tsp oregano

1 bay leaf

salt and black pepper, to taste

Preparation:

Heat a stock pot over medium – high heat. Once the stockpot is hot, add the olive oil, onion, carrots, garlic and herbs. Sauté, stirring occasionally, until the onion is soft and turns translucent (5 – 8 minutes). While the vegetables and herbs are sautéing, cut the chicken thighs into approximately 1" cubes and season with salt and black pepper. Add the seasoned chicken to the pot and cook for an additional 10 minutes, stirring occasionally to prevent burning.
Lower the heat to medium and add the chicken or vegetable stock, water, jalapenos, sweet potato, green onions, Swiss chard and bay leaves and simmer for 20 – 30 minutes, stirring occasionally. Season to taste with lemon juice, salt and black pepper and serve.

Tomato and Zucchini with Curry Sauce

Number of servings: 4

Ingredients:

3 Roma tomatoes, sliced into ½" thick slices
1 medium sized zucchini or yellow squash
1 cup sliced button or crimini mushrooms
2 cloves of garlic, minced
2 tbsp cilantro, chopped finely
5 tbsp coconut oil
salt and black pepper, to taste
The curry sauce:
1 (14 ounce) can of coconut milk
3 tbsp curry powder, or more to taste
2 tbsp honey

Preparation:

The sauce will take longer to prepare than the rest of the dish, so it's a good idea to make this first. Combine the ingredients for the curry sauce in a small saucepan and place over medium – low heat. Mix well and simmer for 20 minutes, stirring occasionally until thickened.

Heat 2 tbsp coconut oil in a large skillet over medium – high heat. Once the oil is hot, add the zucchini slices, taking care not to overlap them; you may find that it's necessary to cook the zucchini in batches, depending on the size of the zucchini and the size of your skillet. Cook for 3 – 4 minutes per side and transfer to a large serving platter.

Heat another 2 tbsp of coconut oil in the skillet and add the tomatoes once the oil is hot. Cook the tomato slices for 3 – 4 minutes per side, gently tossing the skillet as needed to prevent sticking. As with the zucchini, it might be necessary to cook these in two batches. Once they're finished, transfer them to the serving plate on top of the cooked zucchini slices.

Add the last tablespoon of coconut oil to the skillet and once it's hot, add the garlic and mushrooms and cook for about 6 minutes, or until they release their water and become golden brown. Transfer to the serving plate, on top of the tomatoes and zucchini.

Serve the zucchini, tomatoes and mushrooms with the curry sauce on the side – or if you prefer, pour it over the vegetables before serving.

Chicken Salad with Fruit

Number of servings: 3

Ingredients:

1 lb cooked chicken breast
1 cup diced celery
¾ cup grapes (red or green), halved
1 avocado, peeled, seeded and diced
1 apple, cored and diced
1 cup mayonnaise
½ cup chopped walnuts
½ cup dried cranberries
juice of ½ lemon
salt and black pepper, to taste

Preparation:

You can use leftover cooked chicken or cook the chicken
any way you like – roast it, grill it, it doesn't matter as
long as it's cooked. Shred the chicken or chop finely.
Combine with the avocado, dried cranberries, apple,
walnuts and celery in a large bowl and mix well. Mix the
mayonnaise, lemon juice and a little salt and pepper in a
separate bowl. Pour the dressing into the bowl with all

of the other ingredients and mix well to coat the ingredients with the dressing. Place the chicken salad in the refrigerator to chill before serving. Serve over lettuce leaves or baby spinach.

Sweet Potato – Lime Soup

Number of servings: 4

Ingredients:

3 sweet potatoes, cubed (peeling is optional)
4 cups chicken broth or vegetable broth
3 slices of ginger
¾ cup coconut milk
2 lime leaves (omit if you can't find these – they're available at most Asian grocery stores)
½ cup of water
juice of 4 limes or more to taste
2 tbsp chopped cilantro
salt and black pepper, to taste

Preparation:

Add the stock, ginger, lime leaves and sweet potatoes to a large saucepan or stock pot over medium – high heat. Bring to a boil, then reduce to medium – low heat and simmer for 20 – 25 minutes, or until the sweet potatoes are tender enough to easily pierce with a fork.
Remove the ginger and lime leaves and remove the soup from heat and blend until smooth, either with a blender

or a hand held immersion mixer. Return the soup to the saucepan or stock pot and add the lime juice, coconut milk and water; mix well and season to taste with salt and pepper and cook on low heat until heated through. Serve hot topped with chopped cilantro.

Eggplant and Mushroom Curry

Number of servings: 4

Ingredients:

2 large eggplants
4 tomatoes, diced
¼ lb button mushrooms or crimini mushrooms, quartered
1/3 cup coconut milk
2 cloves of garlic, minced
2 green onions, trimmed and sliced thinly
1 tbsp coconut oil
1 Thai chili pepper, finely chopped
1 tbsp chopped cilantro
1 tsp cumin
1 tsp ground coriander
½ tsp turmeric
salt and black pepper, to taste

Preparation:

Start by preheating your oven to 400 F. Wrap the eggplants in foil after piercing them in a few places each with a fork. Once the oven is hot, place them in the oven and bake for 50 – 60 minutes. Remove the eggplants from the oven and allow them to cool until you can handle them without burning yourself. Once the eggplants are cool enough to work with safely, halve them lengthwise and remove the flesh with a spoon. Discard the skins and transfer the flesh to a bowl. Use a fork to break up any large pieces and set aside.

Heat the coconut oil in a large skillet over medium heat. When the oil is hot, add the garlic and sauté, stirring regularly, for about two minutes or until the garlic becomes fragrant. Add the mushrooms, green onion and Thai chili pepper and continue sautéing for another 5 minutes, stirring occasionally. Add the spices, stir well to mix and cook for another 2 – 3 minutes.

Add the tomatoes and simmer for an additional 5 – 7 minutes, or until the tomatoes soften. Add the eggplant, cilantro and coconut milk and continue cooking for another 10 minutes, stirring regularly to break up any remaining large pieces of eggplant and to allow the flavors to combine. Season the curry to taste with salt and black pepper. Serve hot over spaghetti squash or by itself.

Leek and Sweet Potato Soup

Number of servings: 6

Ingredients:

4 large sweet potatoes, cubed (peeling is optional)
2 large leeks, trimmed, sliced in rounds and thoroughly rinsed
4 cups chicken, beef or vegetable stock
1 (14 ounce) can of coconut milk
1 onion, diced
4 cloves of garlic, crushed
1 tbsp coconut oil or ghee
2 tsp cumin
salt and black pepper, to taste

Preparation:

Heat the coconut oil or ghee in a large saucepan over medium heat; when the oil is hot, add the onions and sauté for a few minutes, stirring occasionally until the onions start to turn translucent and soften. Add the leeks and garlic and sauté for another 3 – 5 minutes, until the leeks become tender. Add the cumin and mix well to combine, then add the cubed sweet potatoes and stock. Bring the mixture to a boil briefly and then reduce the heat to medium low. Simmer for 15 – 20 minutes, or until the sweet potatoes become tender.

Red Pepper Dip

Number of servings: 8 – 10

Ingredients:

1 (12 ounce) jar of roasted red peppers, drained
2 cups of walnuts or pecans
2 tbsp mayonnaise
2 tbsp olive oil (use extra virgin olive oil for this recipe, if you have it on hand)
juice of 1 lemon
½ tsp cumin
salt and black pepper, to taste

Preparation:

Add the walnuts or pecans to a food processor or blender and blend until they take on the texture of coarse bread crumbs. Add the mayonnaise, cumin and a little salt and black pepper and blend until well mixed. Add all of the remaining ingredients to your blender or food processor and blend until the mixture reaches your desired consistency (think hummus as far as texture goes). Taste and adjust the seasoning with salt, black pepper and lemon juice. You can serve this right away at room temperature or refrigerate it and serve chilled.

Roasted Beet and Walnut Salad

Number of servings: 4

Ingredients:

4 medium sized beets, scrubbed, ends and stems removed
½ cup chopped walnuts
2 tbsp olive oil (use extra virgin olive oil for this recipe, if you have it on hand)
2 tbsp balsamic vinegar
salt and black pepper, to taste

Preparation:

Preheat your oven to 400 F. Wrap the beets in aluminum foil; once the oven is preheated, place the beets in the oven and roast for about 1 hour, or until the beets are soft enough to pierce easily with a knife. When the beets are cooked, remove them from the oven and allow them to cool until they're safe to handle.

Once the beets are cool enough to handle, remove them from the foil and peel while they're still warm. You may want to wear latex gloves while you do this (if you're using red beets) in order to prevent from staining your hands while you're peeling the beets.

Cube the beets. Transfer to a bowl and add all of the remaining ingredients. Season to taste with salt and black pepper, toss well to coat and allow the beets to sit marinate in the dressing for at least a few minutes before serving. You can also refrigerate the salad for a few hours or overnight before serving in order to allow the flavors to blend.

Asparagus Salad

Number of servings: 4 – 6

Ingredients:

1 lb asparagus, trimmed
1 tbsp minced red onion
1 clove of garlic, minced
1 tbsp olive oil (use extra virgin olive oil for this recipe if you have it on hand)
4 tsp balsamic vinegar or red wine vinegar
salt and black pepper, to taste

Preparation:

Fill a medium sized saucepan halfway full of water and bring to a boil over high heat. Add the asparagus and boil for 3 minutes. Remove the asparagus from heat, drain and rinse under cold water right away to prevent the asparagus from continuing to cook. Pat the asparagus dry with a clean kitchen towel.

Mix together the oil and the balsamic or red wine vinegar. Toss the asparagus with the oil and vinegar and season to taste with salt and black pepper. Season the asparagus to taste with salt and black pepper and serve immediately at room temperature or refrigerate and serve chilled.

Butternut Squash with Thyme

Number of servings: 4

Ingredients:

1 large butternut squash, peeled, seeded and diced into
1/2" cubes
3 cloves of garlic, minced
2 tbsp coconut oil
1 tbsp fresh thyme
salt and black pepper, to taste

Preparation:

Heat a large skillet over medium heat. Once the skillet is
hot, add the coconut oil. Add the cubed squash, garlic
and thyme and stir well. Spread the ingredients out
evenly in the skillet and cook for 3 – 5 minutes without
stirring until the squash is slightly browned. Stir and
cook again without stirring for another 5 minutes. Stir
again, reduce the heat to medium – low, cover and cook
for another 10 – 15 minutes, or until the squash is
tender. Season to taste with salt and black pepper and
serve hot.

Easy Collard Greens

Number of servings: 4

Ingredients:

1 large bunch of collard greens (about 1 lb) washed and patted dry, stems removed
1 small yellow or white onion, diced
3 cloves of garlic, minced
1 Roma tomato, diced
1 tbsp olive oil
salt and black pepper, to taste

Preparation:

Heat a large, heavy skillet over medium – high heat. Once the skillet is hot, add the olive oil. Add the onions and cook, stirring occasionally, until the onions begin to turn translucent. Add the garlic and tomatoes and collard greens and cook, stirring regularly, for another 8 – 10 minutes. Season to taste with salt and black pepper and serve hot.

Steamed Baby Carrots with Dill and Honey

Number of servings: 4 - 6

Ingredients:
4
1 lb baby carrots
1 tbsp honey
1 tbsp coconut oil
2 tbsp fresh dill, chopped finely (or 1 tbsp dried dill)
salt and black pepper, to taste

Preparation:

In a medium sized pot with a steamer basket, bring about 1" of water to a boil. Add the baby carrots to the steamer basket and cover the pot; steam for 15 – 20 minutes, or until the carrots become tender. Remove the carrots from the steamer, add to a bowl. Add the coconut oil, honey and dill and toss to coat. Season the carrots to taste with salt and black pepper and serve at once.

Roasted Cauliflower with Tahini Dressing

Number of servings: 4 – 6

Ingredients:

1 medium sized cauliflower, cored and cut into bite sized florets
½ cup tahini
½ cup water
juice of 1 lemon
2 tbsp olive oil
3 cloves of garlic, crushed
2 tsp cumin
½ tsp nutmeg
a pinch of paprika
½ tsp salt
½ tsp black pepper, or more to taste

Preparation:

Start by preheating your oven to 500 F. Add the cauliflower, olive oil, salt, black pepper and cumin to a large bowl and toss well to coat. Transfer the cauliflower to a baking sheet and spread evenly. Bake for 25 – 35 minutes, or until the cauliflower is tender and browned;

stir a few times while baking.

While the cauliflower is in the oven, mix the tahini, water, crushed garlic, paprika and lemon juice in a bowl. Add a little salt and black pepper to taste. Serve the cauliflower hot or cool to room temperature and serve with the tahini sauce.

Fennel and Carrots

Number of servings: 6

Ingredients:

4 medium sized carrots
2 large bulbs of fennel
2 tbsp coconut oil
salt and black pepper, to taste

Preparation:

Slice the carrots and fennel ¼" to ½" thick. Heat the coconut oil over medium heat in a large skillet. Once the oil is hot, add the vegetables and sauté, stirring occasionally, until the carrots and fennel are tender, about 5- 7 minutes. Season to taste with salt and black pepper and serve.

Kale with Pine Nuts

Number of servings: 4 – 6

Ingredients:

1 lb kale, stems removed and coarsely chopped
2 cloves of garlic, crushed
2 tbsp pine nuts, lightly toasted (you can do this in a dry skillet over medium heat)
1 tbsp olive oil
juice of 1 lemon
salt and black pepper, to taste

Preparation:

Heat the oil in a large, heavy skillet over medium heat. When the oil is hot, add the garlic and cook, stirring occasionally for about 1 minute or until the garlic becomes fragrant. Add the kale and sauté, stirring occasionally, for about 10 minutes or until the kale is tender. Remove from heat, transfer to a serving bowl and add the lemon juice and salt and pepper to taste. Toss to mix and serve, topped with a sprinkling of toasted pine nuts.

Breakfast

Banana – Walnut Muffins

Number of servings: varies (about 6)

Ingredients:

2 bananas
3 eggs
3 dates, pitted
½ cup chopped walnuts, toasted (you can toast the walnuts in a dry skillet over medium heat)
½ cup sugar
¼ cup coconut flour
¼ cup coconut oil
½ tsp baking soda
¼ tsp salt

Preparation:

Preheat your oven to 350 F. Add the bananas, eggs, oil, pitted dates to a food processor and blend until combined. Next, add the coconut flour, baking soda and salt and blend until smooth. Stir in the walnuts. Divide the batter among lined muffin tins and bake for 20 – 25 minutes, or until the tops are browned. Remove from the oven and allow to cool to room temperature before serving.

Eggs with Kale

Number of servings: 2

Ingredients:

4 large eggs
4 kale leaves
a little olive oil for frying
a pinch of salt
black pepper, to taste

Preparation:

Add the kale, eggs and salt to a blender and blend on high speed until smooth while you heat a little olive oil in a skillet over medium heat. Once the oil is hot, pour the egg and kale mixture into the skillet and cook for a minute, then scramble; continue cooking the eggs until they're as done as you prefer them. Serve at once.

Almond Pancakes

Number of servings: 4 – 6 (makes about 18 silver dollar pancakes)

Ingredients:

1 ½ cups almond flour
3 large eggs
2 tbsp honey
1 tbsp water
1 tbsp vanilla extract
¼ tsp baking soda
¼ tsp salt
a little coconut oil, for frying

Preparation:

Add the eggs, water, honey and vanilla extract to a large bowl and whisk to combine. Add the almond flour, baking soda and salt and mix well.
Heat a little coconut oil in a skillet over medium heat. Once the oil is hot, add 1 tbsp of batter per pancake to the skillet. Cook until the tops stop bubbling and flip, then cook the other side. Continue cooking until the batter is used up, adding additional coconut oil to the

skillet as needed. Transfer the cooked pancakes to a plate and cover to keep warm until you're ready to serve.

Spinach Quiche

Number of servings: 4

Ingredients:

6 large eggs
2 cups baby spinach leaves, chopped
½ of a small red onion, diced
1 clove of garlic, minced
½ cup of coconut milk
½ tsp baking powder
salt and black pepper, to taste

Preparation:

Start by preheating your oven to 350 F. While the oven is heating, whisk together the coconut milk and eggs in a large bowl. Add the remaining ingredients, whisking well to combine. Lightly oil a 9" pie dish and pour in the egg mixture. Place the quiche in the oven and bake for about half an hour or until the quiche is cooked through at the center. Remove from the oven, allow to rest for a few minutes, slice and serve.

Cucumber – Blueberry Smoothie

Number of servings: 2 – 4, depending on serving size

Ingredients:

2 large cucumbers, peeled and diced
1 cup frozen blueberries
1 cup of coconut milk
juice of 1 lemon or lime

Preparation:

This is perhaps the easiest recipe in the entire book. Just put all of the ingredients in a blender, blend until smooth and serve.

Cranberry – Almond Bread

Number of servings: varies

Ingredients:

3 large eggs
¾ cup almond butter
½ cup dried cranberries
¼ cup dried apricots, chopped
¼ cup pumpkin seeds
¼ cup sesame seeds
¼ cup sunflower seeds
¼ cup sliced almonds, plus a little extra for topping
¼ cup arrowroot powder
2 tbsp olive oil, plus a little extra for greasing the pan
1 tsp salt
¼ tsp baking soda
a little almond flour, for dusting

Preparation:

Preheat your oven to 350 F. Add the oil, eggs and almond butter to a large bowl and blend until smooth with a hand blender or egg beater. In a separate, small bowl, mix together the arrowroot powder, salt and baking soda; add the arrowroot mixture to the wet ingredients and mix until well combined. Stir in the dried fruits, seeds and nuts.

Oil a loaf pan with olive oil and dust with a little almond flour. Pour the batter into the prepared loaf pan and sprinkle with sliced almonds. Place the pan in the oven and bake for 45 – 50 minutes, or until a knife inserted into the center of the loaf comes out clean. Remove the loaf from the oven and allow to cool for at least one hour before slicing and serving.

Irish Soda Bread

Number of servings: varies

Ingredients:

3 cups almond flour
2 eggs
½ cup raisins
2 tbsp honey
2 tbsp apple cider vinegar
1 ½ tsp baking soda
¼ tsp baking soda
a pinch of caraway seeds

Preparation:

Preheat your oven to 350 F. Combine the almond flour, raisins, salt and baking soda in a large bowl and mix well. In a separate, smaller bowl, whisk together the eggs, honey and vinegar. Add the wet ingredients to the dry ingredients and mix well.

Transfer the dough to a piece of parchment paper and shape into a roughly 8" circular loaf. Score the top of the loaf with a serrated knife in a cross pattern. Sprinkle the top with caraway seeds. Transfer the loaf (still on the parchment paper) to a baking sheet and bake for 20 minutes. Turn off the heat, but leave the loaf in the oven for another 10 minutes before removing. Allow the soda bread to cool for at least 30 minutes. Slice and serve with butter and/or preserves.

Desserts

Chocolate - Avocado Mousse

Number of servings: 8

Ingredients:

The mousse:
4 ripe avocados, peeled and seeded
10 dates, pitted
4 tbsp honey
2 tbsp cacao powder
½ cup pomegranate seeds
The crust:
1 ½ cups walnuts
2 tbsp maple syrup
a pinch of salt

Preparation:

The crust will take longer to make, so start with this part. Add the walnuts to a food processor and grind into small pieces. Add the salt and maple syrup until it forms a coarse dough-like consistency. Add about 2 tbsp of the mixture to 8 ramekins and press into the bottom to form a crust. Transfer the ramekins to the refrigerator to allow the crust to harden.

Place the avocadoes in a food processor, along with the dates, cacao powder and honey. Process the ingredients until completely they are completely smooth. Transfer the mouse into a piping bag (you can make your own by adding the mousse to a ziplock bag and cutting off one corner).
Remove the ramekins from the refrigerator and pipe the mousse into the ramekins. Return the ramekins to the refrigerator and chill for at least 1 hour. Serve cold, garnished with pomegranate seeds.

Chocolate – Cranberry Pie

Number of servings: 6 - 8

Ingredients:

The crust:
2 cups almond flour
1 egg
2 tbsp coconut oil
½ tsp salt
The filling and toppings:
1 lb frozen cranberries (about 2 cups)
½ cup coconut milk
8 ounces dark chocolate (70% cocoa)
½ cup sugar

Preparation:

Start by preheating your oven to 375 F while you make the crust. Add all of the ingredients to a blender and process until they form a crumbly dough (much like traditional pastry dough). Lightly grease a 9" pie dish and transfer the dough into the prepared dish. Use your hands to press the dough evenly over the bottom of the pie dish.

Place the crust in the oven and bake for about 15 minutes, or until it turns golden brown and flaky. Remove the crust from the oven and allow it to cool to room temperature.

You can start making the filling while the crust bakes. Pour the coconut milk into a small saucepan and bring to a boil over medium – high heat. Once it reaches a boil, remove from heat at once and add the chocolate and 1/4 cup of sugar. Stir continuously until the chocolate melts completely and is combined with the coconut milk. Pour the filling into the cooled pie shell and transfer the pie to the refrigerator. Chill for at least 2 hours and for as long as 24 hours to allow the filling to solidify.

Preheat your oven to 375 F. Once the oven is hot, spread the cranberries on a baking sheet, sprinkle with ¼ cup of sugar and bake for about 10 minutes, stirring once or twice to prevent them from sticking. When the cranberries are soft and starting to blister, remove from heat and transfer them to a bowl. Refrigerate the cranberries for at least 1 hour. Spoon the cooled cranberries on top of the pie, slice and serve.

Paleo Style Coconut Cream Pie

Number of servings: 6 – 8

Ingredients:

The crust:
3 large eggs
2 ounces dark chocolate (85% - 90% cacao)
¾ cup coconut flour
½ cup coconut flakes
¼ cup coconut oil
2 tbsp cold water (or more, if necessary)
2 tbsp coconut sugar (or sugar, if you can't find coconut sugar)
1 tsp vanilla extract
¼ tsp baking soda
¼ tsp salt
The filling:
4 egg yolks from large eggs
2 cans (14 ounces) coconut milk
2/3 cup creamed coconut
2/3 cup coconut sugar (or sugar, if you can't find coconut sugar)
9 tbsp arrowroot powder
1 tsp vanilla extract

¼ tsp salt
The topping:
½ cup coconut flakes
dark chocolate shavings

Preparation:

Preheat your oven to 325 F. Add the coconut flakes and coconut flour to a food processor and pulse until thoroughly combined. Whisk together the coconut oil, eggs, salt, coconut sugar, vanilla extract and baking soda in a medium sized bowl. Add the egg mixture to the dry ingredients in the food processor and pulse until the mixture forms a crumbly, pastry dough – like mixture. Add the water very slowly until the dough comes together and is slightly moist.

Spread the dough with your hands in a 9" pie dish to form a crust. Place in the oven and bake the crust for 15 minutes, or until it is golden brown. Remove from the oven and allow it to cool completely. Melt the chocolate in a microwave or in a double boiler. Brush the cooled pie shell with melted chocolate. Transfer the pie shell to the refrigerator to allow the chocolate to harden.

Add ice cubes and cold water to a large bowl and set it aside. In a medium sized bowl, whisk the egg yolks and set aside. Add the coconut milk, creamed coconut, coconut sugar, salt and vanilla extract to a saucepan and bring to a simmer. Cook for about 10 minutes, whisking constantly to prevent separation. The mixture will thicken as it cooks. Whisk ¼ of the coconut milk mixture into the egg yolks, then add the remainder of the mixture and whisk well to combine.

Return the coconut milk and egg mixture to the saucepan and cook over medium- high heat, whisking constantly until it thickens and bubbles start to form in the center of the custard (about 10 minutes). Pour the custard into a medium sized bowl and transfer the bowl into the ice bath. Allow the custard to cool for 30 – 40 minutes, whisking occasionally. Add the arrowroot powder and whisk until combined and slightly thickened. Place a sheet of plastic wrap on the surface of the custard (this will prevent a skin from forming on your custard) and transfer to the refrigerator. Chill for at least 4 hours and for as long as 24 hours to allow the custard to thicken.

Toast the coconut flakes in a dry skillet over medium heat, stirring occasionally and set aside. Remove the pie shell from the refrigerator and fill with the custard, using a spatula to spread it evenly. Return the pie to the refrigerator and chill for at least 3 hours. Garnish with toasted coconut flakes and dark chocolate shavings, slice and serve.

Pineapple – Coconut Frozen Custard

Number of servings: varies depending on serving sizes

Ingredients:

¾ cup finely chopped fresh pineapple
1 (14 ounce) can coconut milk
4 egg yolks
¼ cup pineapple juice
3 tbsp honey
1 tbsp vanilla extract

Preparation:

Note: You'll need an ice cream maker to make this recipe.
Add the pineapple juice, coconut milk, vanilla extract and honey to a medium sized saucepan and bring to a simmer over medium – low heat.

While the coconut milk and pineapple juice mixture is heating, whisk the egg yolks in a small bowl until they're frothy. Pour ¼ of the hot coconut milk and pineapple juice mixture into the eggs, whisking as you add it in. Pour this mixture into the saucepan and whisk to combine. Return the mixture to a simmer, whisking constantly until the mixture thickens slightly – this will take about 5 minutes.

Transfer to a bowl and refrigerate until cool. Once the mixture is cooled, pour into an electric ice cream maker and proceed according to the manufacturer's directions. A few minutes before it's done, add the chopped pineapple. When the machine completes the process, you can eat your frozen custard right away, but it will be fairly soft. For a harder ice cream, freeze the custard for a few hours before serving.

About the Recipes Contained in this Book

These recipes were selected to be suitable for the diet and lifestyle discussed in this book. Although we create our own recipes, we also do like to give credit to the amazing chefs who inspired our work. Some recipes may be adapted from other popular recipes on the internet or other sources. We would like to give credit and thanks for this.

The book presents our favorites and the recipes we feel fit the topic best in order to provide the highest quality experience for our highly valued readers.

Paleo Cookbook Conclusion

There's no getting around the fact that like any kind of diet, the Paleo diet does limit what you can eat in certain ways – but as you can see from the wide variety of recipes in this cookbook, you definitely don't have to feel deprived when you take up this diet. However, there are some very important differences between this and the fad diets which seem to come and go in a matter of weeks or months.

Unlike fad diets, the Paleo diet isn't just a diet; it's a lifestyle which ideally incorporates diet and exercise into a harmonious whole which leads to better health and meals which are every bit as delicious – if not more so – than anything you were eating before. In fact, many of the recipes here are simply healthier variations on dishes which you already enjoy. Once you get used to living without processed foods and going light on the dairy and sugar, you won't miss eating a conventional modern diet one bit!

Using the recipes and ideas found in this book as a sort of template, you can and should feel free to experiment in the kitchen. Substitute grains with healthier choices like spaghetti squash or zucchini noodles for pasta and almond flour for wheat flour, reduce the amount of sugar you eat and wherever possible, replace it with honey or maple syrup and you'll be well on your way to coming up with some new, Paleo-friendly, healthy and most important of all, delicious culinary creations of your very own. There are only a few rules in the Paleo diet and aside from these, your imagination is the only limit to what you can come up with!

Section 2: Grain Free Diet

What are the benefits of eating a grain free diet? Normally people who go on a grain free diet are ones who suffer from grain allergies and intolerances. Unfortunately, many do suffer from such issues. Really, the issues are with the protein of the grain, the gluten. Grains are found in breads, pastas, and flours and come from corn, barley, wheat, oats and bajra. Another grain is rice, but rice does not contain gluten. Rice is not a protein it is a starch. Rice is included in this grain free diet book since it is not gluten. The replacement for grains comes from foods like peas and legumes (beans), soy, and nuts. But when people refer to a grain free diet they literally mean a wheat free diet, or a diet that is gluten free. Some of the recipes within this book do contain corn and oats, but none of the recipes contains wheat or gluten. With this in mind, always check the ingredients for any foods on the ingredient lists of these recipes. Some foods may sneak in wheat products so make sure you are using wheat free foods.

A grain free diet will help to clear away many digestive issues. Digestive disorders are the main symptom of gluten intolerances and allergies. These disorders can be so bad it leaves people helpless and chained to their restrooms. The good news is that by eliminating grains from their diet they are able to overcome and treat these digestive conditions to the point of restoring a normal life.

The better alternative to grains is fruits and vegetables. The human body does need fiber and fruits and vegetables contain a high level of healthy natural fiber. The fiber from fruits and vegetables are high in nutrients, which helps the body to build strong immune systems.

Try the recipes and feel free to improvise with them. Substitute ingredients and see if you can come up with your own unique version. Many of the recipes call for fruits and vegetables and these are easy to substitute. Cut the recipes in half if you need less and double or triple if you need more. Most of these recipes are easy to use, easy to read and made with ingredients that are readily available and easy to find.

Breakfast Recipes

Oven Baked Omelet

If you love eggs, you will love this oven baked omelet, which is a full meal all by itself. It is delicious for breakfast, lunch, or supper.

Makes 8 servings.

Ingredients:

*6 eggs
*1 potato (baking or large russet)
*1 tomato (sliced thin)
*1/2 cup of onion (chopped)
*1/2 cup of ham (chopped)
*1/4 cup of cheddar cheese (shredded)
*1/4 cup of red bell pepper (chopped)
*1/4 cup of mushrooms (chopped)
*1/4 cup of parsley (fresh chopped)
*2 tablespoons of olive oil
*1 teaspoon of salt
*1/2 teaspoon of pepper (black ground)

Directions:

Boil the potato until it is tender but not mushy about 15

to 20 minutes. Peel it and slice it.

Turn oven to 350 degrees Fahrenheit for the omelet.
Add the 6 eggs to a bowl and beat. Stir in the 1/4 cup of
fresh chopped parsley, teaspoon of salt and 1/2
teaspoon of pepper. Pour the 2 tablespoons of olive oil
into a large oven safe skillet and turn the heat to
medium high. Add the 1/2 cup of chopped onions and
1/4 cup of chopped red bell peppers and sauté. Next,
add the 1/4 cup of mushrooms, then the sliced potato,
sliced tomato and the 1/2 cup of chopped ham. When
the mushrooms have shrunk, turn the stove off. Pour
the egg mixture into the same skillet and stir. Sprinkle
the 1/4 cup of shredded cheddar cheese over the top
and place the skillet in the hot oven. Bake for about 12
minutes. Cool slightly then serve.

Flapjacks

A delicious hot breakfast, serves up well with butter (or margarine) and maple syrup or your favorite fruit toppings.

Makes a dozen flapjacks.

Ingredients:

*1 1/2 cups of almond flour (blanched)
*1/2 cup of water
*1/4 cup of agave nectar
*2 eggs
*1 tablespoon of vanilla extract
*1/2 teaspoon of salt
*1/2 teaspoon of baking soda
*canola oil

Add the 1/2 cup of water, 1/4 cup of agave nectar, 2 eggs, and the 1 tablespoon of vanilla extract in a bowl and beat with electric beaters until completely smooth. Add the 1 1/2 cups of blanched almond flour, 1/2 teaspoon of salt and 1/2 teaspoon of baking soda in a bowl and mix and then slowly add to the batter and beat for a few minutes longer until all ingredients are incorporated. Add a little canola oil to the skillet and heat to medium. Pour ladels of flapjack batter onto the hot skillet and cook until the bubbles form. Gently flip the flapjack to brown the other side, takes just a minute or two. Cook until all are done. Top as desired and serve hot.

Pancakes

A favorite breakfast for the family without using wheat.

Makes 8 servings.

Ingredients:

*2 1/2 cups of yogurt
*2 cups of rice flour (sweet)
*1/2 cup of rice milk
*4 eggs
*4 tablespoons of canola oil
*4 teaspoons of baking powder
*1 teaspoon of baking soda
*1 teaspoon of cinnamon (ground)
*1 teaspoon of salt

Directions:

Add the 2 cups of sweet rice flour to a bowl along with the 4 teaspoons of baking powder, teaspooons of baking soda, ground cinnamon, and salt. In a separate bowl crack the 4 eggs and beat. Then add the 2 1/2 cups of yogurt, 1/2 cup of rice milk and the 4 tablespoons of canola oil. Gradually stir into the flour bowl, careful not to over stir, batter may be slightly lumpy. Add a little canola oil to a skillet or a griddle and heat to medium high. Pour a ladle full of batter and cook until the edges bubble. Carefully flip and cook to a golden brown on both sides. Top with your favorite pancake toppings.

Pecan Granola Crunch

Just because you are going grain free doesn't mean you can't enjoy a nice treat with pecan granola.

Makes 8 servings.

Ingredients:

*1 cup of pecans (chopped)
*1 cup of dates (chopped)
*1 cup of sunflower seeds
*1 cup of coconut (shredded and unsweetened)
*1/4 cup of maple syrup
*1/4 cup of applesauce
*1 teaspoon of vanilla extract

Directions:

Prep: Preheat oven to 325 degrees Fahrenheit. Line a baking sheet with parchment paper.

Combine the cup of chopped pecans, chopped dates, sunflower seeds and shredded coconut in a large bowl. In a separate bowl, mix the 1/4 cup of maple syrup, 1/4 cup of applesauce and teaspoon of vanilla extract. Pour over the nut mixture and toss to coat. Spread the granola over the lined baking sheet. Bake for 15 minutes, then flip the pieces so it gives an even golden brown and bake for another 15 minutes and allow to cool completely before eating. Store in an airtight container.

Coconut Blueberry Crepes

Crepes come in more than just one flavor. This particular recipe features blueberries and coconuts.

Makes 6 servings.

Ingredients:

*1 1/2 cups of blueberries
*1/3 cup of coconut milk
*2 eggs
*2 tablespoons of coconut flour
*2 tablespoons of coconut oil
*1/4 teaspoon of vanilla extract
*1/8 teaspoon of salt
*pinch of cinnamon (ground)
*pinch of nutmeg (ground)
*confectioners' sugar (for dusting)
*cooking spray

Directions:

Add the eggs to a bowl and beat. Mix in the 2 tablespoons of coconut oil (melted first), 1/4 teaspoon of vanilla and the 1/8 teaspoon of salt. Stir in the 2 tablespoons of coconut flour, pinches of ground cinnamon and nutmeg. Add the 1/3 cup of coconut milk and mix well.

Spray with cooking spray then heat the griddle or a skillet on medium heat. Pour a small ladle full of crepe batter in hot surface, allowing it to spread out to about half a foot around. Cook for 90 seconds, then gently flip and cook the other side for 90 seconds. Spoon the blueberries on the crepe and roll. Dust with confectioners' sugar and serve.

Muffins

Cherry Cordial Muffins

This is a delicious grain free muffin with cherries and semisweet chocolate chips, not your average muffin at all.

Makes two dozen muffins.

Ingredients:

*4 cups of rice flour (white)
*2 bananas (ripe)
*1 1/2 cups of soy milk (vanilla)
*1 cup of applesauce
*1 cup of cherries (dried)
*1 cup of semisweet chocolate chips
*4 eggs
*4 tablespoons of canola oil
*2 tablespoon of brown sugar
*1 1/2 teaspoon of baking powder
*1/2 teaspoon of salt

Directions:

Prep: Preheat oven to 400 degrees Fahrenheit. Line 2 muffin tins with cupcake liners.

Mash the 2 ripe bananas and place in a bowl along with

the 1 1/2 cups of vanilla soy milk, cup of applesauce, 4 tablespoons of canola oil and the 2 tablespoons of brown sugar. Mix well. Beat the 4 eggs and stir into the batter. In a separate bowl mix the 4 cups of white rice flour with the 1 1/2 teasoons of baking powder and 1/2 teaspoon of salt. Gradually add the dry ingredients into the batter. Fold in the cup of dried cherries and the cup of semisweet chocolate chips. Spoon evenly into 24 lined muffin tins. Bake until tops are a golden brown, about half an hour.

Macadamia Fruit Muffins

If you like the flavors of macadamia coupled with coconut and banana, you will love this delicious muffin.

Makes a dozen muffins.

Ingredients:

*1 cup of almond flour (blanched)
*2/3 cup of macadamia nuts (chopped)
*2/3 cup of coconut flakes (shredded unsweetened)
*1/3 cup of honey
*1/3 cup of coconut oil (melted, but cool)
*1/4 cup of coconut flour
*3 bananas (very ripe)
*2 eggs
*1 teaspoon of lemon juice
*1 teaspoon of vanilla extract
*3/4 teaspoon of baking soda
*1/2 teaspoon of salt

Directions:

Prep: Preheat the oven to 350 degrees Fahrenheit. Place cupcake liners in 12 muffin tins.

Spread the 2/3 cup of chopped macadamia nuts and the 2/3 cup of shredded unsweetened coconut flakes onto a cookie sheet and toast for about 7 minutes, stir them twice during this time.

Mix the cup of blanched almond flour with the 1/4 cup of coconut flour, 3/4 teaspoon of baking soda and 1/2 teaspoon of salt. In a separate bowl add the 2 eggs and beat. Stir in the 1/3 cup of honey, teaspoons of lemon juice and vanilla extract. Peel and mash the 3 ripe bananas and stir into the batter. Gradually add the dry ingredients, mixing well. Fold in the toasted nuts and coconut. Evenly spoon the batter into the 12 lined muffin tins. Bake until tops turn golden brown, about half an hour.

Nutty Banana Muffins

A delicious banana muffin made with pecans and coconut.

Makes a dozen muffins.

Ingredients:

*1/2 cup of coconut flour
*1/2 cup of pecans (finely chopped)
*1/3 cup of coconut flakes
*1/3 cup of coconut oil (melted)
*1/3 cup of honey
*6 eggs
*2 bananas (very ripe)
*1 tablespoon of vanilla extract
*1/2 teaspoon of salt
*1/2 teaspoon of baking soda

Directions:

Prep: Preheat the oven to 350 degrees Fahrenheit. Place cupcake linters in 12 muffin tins.

Combine the 1/2 cup of coconut flour, 1/2 teaspoon of salt and 1/2 teaspoon of baking soda. In a seperate bowl add the 6 eggs and beat, then mix in the 1/3 cup of melted coconut oil, 1/3 cup of honey and the tablespoon of vanilla extract. Mash the 2 very ripe bananas and mix into the batter. Gradually add the dry ingredients. Fold in the 1/2 cups of coconut flakes and finely chopped pecans. Evenly spoon the batter into the 12 lined muffin tins. Bake until tops are golden brown, about 25 minutes.

Banana Nut Muffins

Nothing smells better in the morning than fresh banana muffins baking.

Makes a dozen muffins.

Ingredients:

*1 cup of coconut flour
*1/2 cup of pecans (finely chopped)
*6 eggs
*2 bananas (very ripe)
*4 tablespoons of coconut oil (melted)
*2 tablespoons of coconut milk
*2 tablespoons of honey
*1 teaspoon of baking powder
*1/2 teaspoon of vanilla extract
*1/8 teaspoon of salt

Directions:

Prep: Preheat the oven to 350 degrees Fahrenheit. Place cupcake liners in 12 muffin tins.

Mix the 1 cup of coconut flour with the teaspoon of baking powder and 1/8 teaspoon of salt. In a separate bowl add the 6 eggs and beat, and then stir in the 4 tablespoons of coconut milk, 2 tablespoons of honey and 1/2 teaspoon of vanilla extract. Mash the 2 bananas and add them to the batter, mixing well. Gradually add the dry ingredients and stir until blended. Fold in the finely chopped pecans. Spoon evenly in the 12 lined muffin tins. Bake until tops are golden brown about 20 minutes.

Alternative, leave out the pecans. Substitute with walnuts.

Lemon Cran-Co-Nut Muffins

Combine the three flavors of lemon, cranberry and coconut and you have this delicious sweet muffin.

Makes a dozen muffins.

Ingredients:

*1 cup of cranberries
*3/4 cup of coconut flour
*1/2 cup of coconut oil (melted)
*1/4 cup of maple syrup
*1/4 cup of coconut (unsweetened shredded)
*7 eggs
*1 lemon (zest and the juice)
*2 teaspoons of vanilla extract
*1 teaspoon of baking powder
*1/2 teaspoon of salt

Directions:

Prep: Preheat oven to 350 degrees Fahrenheit. Place cupcake liners in 12 muffin tins.

Mix the 3/4 cup of coconut flour with the teaspoon of baking powder and 1/2 teaspoon of salt. In a separate bowl beat the 7 eggs then stir in the 1/2 cup of melted coconut oil, 1/4 cup of maple syrup, zest and juice of 1 lemon and the 2 teaspoons of vanilla extract. Gradually stir in the dry ingredients. Fold in the cup of cranberries and the 1/4 cup of shredded unsweetened coconut. Spoon evenly in the dozen lined muffin tins. Bake until tops turn golden brown, about 20 minutes.

Blackberryana Muffins

The moist flavor of bananas combined with the tangy sweetness of blackberries makes for a delightful treat.

Makes a dozen muffins.

Ingredients:

*2 cups of coconut oil (melted)
*1 cup of blackberries
*3/4 cup of coconut flour
*8 eggs
*2 bananas (very ripe)
*5 tablespoons of maple syrup
*3 teaspoons of cinnamon (ground)
*2 teaspoons of vanilla extract
*1 teaspoon of baking powder
*1/2 teaspoon of salt

Blackberryana Muffins

The moist flavor of bananas combined with the tangy sweetness of blackberries makes for a delightful treat.

Makes a dozen muffins.

Ingredients:

*2 cups of coconut oil (melted)
*1 cup of blackberries
*3/4 cup of coconut flour
*8 eggs
*2 bananas (very ripe)
*5 tablespoons of maple syrup
*3 teaspoons of cinnamon (ground)
*2 teaspoons of vanilla extract
*1 teaspoon of baking powder
*1/2 teaspoon of salt

Directions:

Prep: Preheat oven to 350 degrees Fahrenheit. Place cupcake liners in 12 muffin tins.

Mix the 3/4 cup of coconut flour with teaspoon of baking powder, 3 teaspoons of ground cinnamon, and 1/2 teaspoon of salt. Set aside. In a separate bowl add the 8 eggs and beat. Stir in the 5 tablespoons of maple syrup and the 2 teaspoons of vanilla extract. Mash the 2 very ripe bananas and stir into the batter. Stir in the 2 cups of melted coconut oil. Gradually add the dry ingredients. Fold in the cup of blackberries. Spoon evenly into the 12 lined muffin tins. Bake until golden brown, about 23 minutes.

Cinnamon Roll Muffins

The lovely aroma of cinnamon baking will bring everyone to the kitchen for a sample.

Makes a dozen muffins.

Ingredients:

*2 1/2 cups of almond flour
*1/2 cup of coconut milk (+ 1 tablespoon)
*1/2 cup of honey (+2 tablespoons)
*2 eggs
*1 tablespoon of coconut flour
*1 tablespoon of cinnamon (ground) (+1 teaspoon)
*1 tablespoon of coconut oil (melted)
*1/2 teaspoon of baking soda
*1/4 teaspoon of salt

Directions:

Prep: Preheat oven to 325 degrees Fahrenheit. Add cupcake liners to 12 muffin tins.

Add the 2 1/2 cups of almond flour in with the tablespoon of coconut flour, 1 teaspoon of ground cinnamon, 1/2 teaspoon of baking soda, and 1/4 teaspoon of salt and stir. In a separate bowl, add the 2 eggs and beat, then mix in the 1/2 cup and tablespoon of coconut milk and 1/2 cup of honey. Gradually add the

dry ingredients and mix.   Spoon evenly into the 12 lined
muffin tins. In a separate bowl, mix the 2 tablespoons of
honey with the 1 tablespoon of melted coconut oil and
the tablespoon of ground cinnamon. Drizzle this over
the tops of the 12 filled muffin tins. Bake until tops are
golden brown, about 23 minutes.

Spicy Banana Bread Muffins

This banana bread is moist and delicious with a coconut twist.

Makes 12 muffins.

Ingredients:

*8 eggs (beaten)
*2 bananas (very ripe)
*3/4 cup of coconut flour
*1/2 cup of coconut oil (melted)
*1/2 cup of coconut (shredded)
*5 tablespoons of honey
*5 teaspoons of cinnamon (ground)
*2 teaspoons of vanilla extract
*1/2 teaspoon of salt

Directions:

Prep: Preheat oven to 350 degrees Fahrenheit. Place cupcake liners into 12 muffin tins.

Mix the 3/4 cup of coconut flour with the 5 teaspoons of ground cinnamon and 1/2 teaspoon of salt. In a separate bowl mash the 2 bananas then add the 8 beaten eggs, 1/2 cup of melted coconut oil, 1/2 cup of shredded coconut, 5 tablespoons of honey and the 2 teaspoons of vanilla extract and mix well. Add the flour mixture stirring until combined. Spoon evenly into the 12 lined muffin tins. Bake until it is golden brown, about half an hour.

Blueberry Muffins

Delicious blueberry muffins are good warm with a pat of butter or margarine. Warm in a microwave for 15 seconds if they have cooled.

Makes a dozen muffins.

Ingredients:

*2 1/2 cups of almond flour
*1 cup of blueberries
*1/4 cup of honey
*3 eggs
*1 tablespoon of vanilla extract
*1/2 teaspoon of baking powder
*1/2 teaspoon of salt

Prep: Preheat oven to 300 degrees Fahrenheit. Add cupcake liners to a dozen muffin tins, or spray each tin with cooking spray.

Add the 2 1/2 cups of almond flour with the 1/2 teaspoon of baking powder and 1/2 teaspoon of salt. Mix and set aside. Crack the 3 eggs in a separate bowl and beat. Add the 1/4 cup of honey and the tablespoon of vanilla extract and mix. Add the liquid to the dry ingredients and stir. Fold in the cup of blueberries, carefully. Spoon evenly into the 12 muffin tins and bake for about 35 minutes until the tops are a golden brown.

Cool slightly before serving.

Pumpkin Spice Muffins

Everyone loves muffins and these are spicy and moist.
Makes 20 muffins

Ingredients:

*2 1/4 cups of buckwheat flour
*2 cups of pumpkin (puree)
*1 1/4 cups of sugar (granulated)
*1 cup of buttermilk
*1 cup of raisins
*1/2 cup of canola oil
*3 eggs
*1 teaspoon of vanilla extract
*1 teaspoon of baking powder
*1 teaspoon of baking soda
*1 teaspoon of cinnamon (ground)
*1/2 teaspoon of cloves (ground)
*1/2 teaspoon of ginger (ground)

Directions:

Prep: Preheat oven to 350 degrees Fahrenheit. Add
cupcake liners to 20 muffin tins.

Add the 3 eggs to a bowl and beat. Pour in the 1 1/4 cups of granulated sugar, cup of buttermilk, 1/2 cup of canola oil, and the teaspoon of vanilla extract. Mix well. Add the 2 cups of pumpkin puree and beat with an electric mixer for a minute or two. In a separate bowl, add the 2 1/4 cups of buckwheat flour with the teaspoons of baking powder, baking soda, and ground cinnamon and the 1/2 teaspoons of ground cloves and ground ginger. Mix well. Fold in the cup of raisins. Divide by spoon into the 20 lined muffin cups. Bake until golden brown, about 20 minutes.

Main Dish

Chicken Nuggets

Children especially love these delicious nuggets, they make a great meat for the main meal or work well as a snack or appetizer.
Makes approximately 48 chicken nuggets.

Ingredients:

*8 chicken breasts fillets (halves)
*1 cup of leeks (chopped)
*1 cup of onions (chopped)
*1/2 cup of celery (chopped)
*1 small carrot (peeled and chopped)
*canola oil to cover skillet bottom (for frying)
*1/2 tablespoon of quinoa flour + sprinkle
*1 teaspoon of salt

Directions:

Add the cup of chopped leeks, cup of chopped onions, 1/2 cup of chopped celery and the small peeled and chopped carrot into a blender or food processor. Dice into fine bits. Cut the 8 chicken breast fillets into chunks and add to the vegetable mixture in the processor. Also add the 1/2 tablespoon of quinoa flour and teaspoon of salt. Turn to mince until the entire mixture is minced. Add a sprinkling of quinoa flour to a bowl. Form "nuggets" from the chicken mixture and roll in the flour. Pour the canola oil to about half an inch in the skillet and heat. Drop the chicken nuggets into the oil and fry until all sides reach a nice golden brown and well done. Place on paper towels or a rack to drain the grease and cool a couple of minutes before serving.

Serving suggestion: Dip in honey mustard, barbecue sauce, ranch dressing or gravy.

Chicken Parmesan

A delicious Italian favorite. Serve with a salad and steamed veggies.

Makes 12 servings.

Ingredients:

*4 chicken breasts (boneless and skinless)
*4 cups of mozzarella cheese (shredded)
*2 cups of almond flour (blanched)
*2 cups of water
*2 eggs (beaten)
*14 ounces of tomato paste
*6 tablespoons of olive oil
*6 teaspoons of garlic (minced fresh)
*1 teaspoon of Herbes de Provence

Directions:

Prep: Preheat oven to 400 degrees Fahrenheit.

Cut each chicken breast into thirds lengthwise. Wash then pat dry with a paper towel. Beat the 2 eggs in a bowl and drag the chicken cuts through the egg. Add the 2 cups of blanched almond flour onto a plate or platter. Coat each chicken strip with the almond flour. Add the 6 tablespoons of olive oil to a skillet and heat to medium. Place the chicken strips into the hot oil and cook until they reach a crispy golden brown, on each side. Place hot chicken strips on a wire rack or a plate lined with paper towels. In a smaller saucepan add the 14 ounces of tomato paste along with the 2 cups of water, 6 teaspoons of minced garlic and teaspoon of Herbes de Provence. Stir and simmer for about 15 minutes. In an 11x7 baking dish, spread a couple serving spoons of sauce, enough to cover the bottom. Add the chicken and pour the remaining sauce over the top. Sprinkle the mozzarella cheese over the top and bake for 10 minutes in the preheated oven. Serve immediately.

Breaded Chicken Tenders

A favorite for sure, tasty, and crispy chicken tenders.

Makes 6 servings.

Ingredients:

*2 large chicken breasts (boneless and skinless, cut into 6 strips)
*1 cup of almond flour
*1 cup of Parmesan cheese (finely grated)
*1/2 cup of butter (melted)
*1/2 teaspoon of basil (dried)
*1/2 teaspoon of thyme (dried)
*salt and pepper to season

Directions:

Prep: Preheat oven to 375 degrees Fahrenheit. Either spray a baking sheet with cooking spray, or line it with foil.

Mix the cup of almond flour with the cup of finely grated Parmesan cheese, 1/2 teaspoons of dried basil, dried thyme and dashes of salt and pepper. Run the chicken strips through the 1/2 cup of melted butter, then roll through the almond flour and Parmesan cheese mixture, coating well. Place the coated chicken strips on the baking sheet. Bake until the outside turns a gold brown. Make sure the center of the strips are not pink but well done (test one strip). Baking takes about 20 minutes. Serve hot.

Spaghetti and Sauce With Meat

Enjoy a delicious Italian inspired spaghetti dish without using grains.

Makes 8 servings.

Ingredients for noodles:

*4 zucchinis (medium size)
*2 tablespoons of olive oil (extra virgin)
*1 teaspoon of salt
*water

Directions for noodles:

Create the zucchini noodles by "peeling" each layers at a time, all the way down to the seedy middle. Peel in "thin" strips to mimic spaghetti noodles. Add the "noodles" in a bowl and cover with cold water. Sprinkle the teaspoon of salt over the top. Set aside for 30 minutes. Make the meat sauce below. After the soak, drain the water and place noodles in a paper towel - spread out. Add a paper towel on top and gently roll to dry the zucchini noodles completely. Next, add 2 tablespoons of extra virgin olive oil in a skillet and turn to medium heat. Once the oil is hot, add the zucchini noodles and sauté for no longer than 3 minutes. Remove immediately and wait for the sauce.

Ingredients for spaghetti sauce:

*1 1/2 pound of ground beef
*4 cups of chicken stock
*2 cans of tomato paste
*1 cup of onions (chopped)
*4 garlic cloves (chopped)
*4 tablespoons of Italian Seasoning
*Pamesan cheese (to season)
*parsley (to garnish)

Directions for spaghetti sauce:

Add the ground beef in a skillet and brown, then add the 1 cup of chopped onions while the beef is cooking. Drain the grease and set aside. Add the 4 cups of chicken stock, 2 cans of tomato paste, 4 chopped garlic cloves and 4 tablespoons of Italian Seasoning to a food processor or blender and blend until it is well mixed. Pour the tomato mixture into the cooked ground beef and onions. Turn the heat to low and simmer for 20 minutes, covered. Once the sauce is done, divide the zucchini noodles on 8 plates (or less with larger portions) and spoon the sauce over, just like spaghetti. Top with Parmesan cheese and garnish with parsley and enjoy.

Chicken and Dumplings

This timeless recipe is hearty and delicious and the best of comfort foods.

Makes 8 servings.

Ingredients:

*1 chicken (whole)
*48 ounces of chicken stock
*water
*1 cup of pecan meal
*1/4 cup of arrowroot
*1/4 cup of powdered milk
*1/4 cup of rice flour
*3 eggs
*6 tablespoons of canola oil
*1 teaspoon of honey
*salt and pepper to season

Directions:

Rinse the chicken and place in a large stock pot. Pour the 48 ounce can of chicken stock over the chicken and add enough water to submerge the chicken. Boil the chicken on high heat until it is done (no more pink) about half an hour. Check and when the meat is no longer pink it is done.

Remove the chicken - keep the chicken stock and water in the pot. Pick all the skin off and discard. Pull off the meat and discard all of the bones. Chop the meat and return to the stock pot, turn heat to medium. In a bowl, make the dumplings, mix the 1 cup of pecan meal, 1/4 cup of arrowroot, 3 eggs, and the teaspoon of honey. Sprinkle salt and pepper and stir. Set aside for a minute. Add 1/4 cup of rice flour and the 1/4 cup of powdered milk to the chicken and stock liquid. Stir and turn heat to medium. Season with salt and pepper. Drop spoonfuls of the dumplings into the hot chicken stock. Put a lid on and turn heat to low. Simmer for about half an hour. Cool a little before serving.

Lasagna

Who says just because you are eating grain free you can't enjoy a delicious lasagna.

Makes 8 servings.

Ingredients:

*1 can of crushed tomatoes (28 oz.)
*1 can of tomato paste (6 oz.)
*2 eggplants (sliced into "lasagna noodles", about a quarter inch thick)
*1 3/4 cups of ricotta cheese
*1 cup of carrots (shredded)
*1 cup of spinach (frozen and chopped)
*1 cup of mozzarella cheese (shredded)
*1/2 cup of onions (diced)
*1/2 cup of Romano cheese (freshly grated)
*2 eggs
*2 tablespoons of salt + 1/2 teaspoon
*3 tablespoons of olive oil + 1 teaspoon
*1 teaspoon of oregano (dried)
*1 teaspoon of basil (dried)
*2 teaspoons of onion (powder)
*2 teaspoons of garlic (powder)
*salt and pepper to season

Directions:

Lay the eggplant slices out over paper towels and sprinkle with 1 tablespoon of salt. Turn the slices over and sprinkle the other side. Lay paper towels over the top of the slices, then set heavy baking dishes or pots on top of the towels. This helps to wick out the moisture and dry the eggplant. This process takes about 60 minutes. Afterwards, discard the paper towels and rinse the eggplant in cold water, dry with new paper towels. Next, add 2 tablespoons of olive oil to a skillet and heat on medium. Fry the eggplant slices in single layers for around 4 minutes, flip and 4 minutes on each side. Put the fried eggplant slices on a paper towel lined platter. In a bowl add the 28 ounce can of crushed tomatoes, 6 oz. can of tomato paste, teaspoon of dried oregano, teaspoon of dried basil, teaspoon of onion powder, teaspoon of garlic powder and dashes of salt and pepper and mix well. Next, add the teaspoon of olive oil to the skillet, turn to medium heat and add the 1/2 cup of diced onions and sauté. Add the cup of shredded carrots and the cup of frozen chopped spinach and cook and stir for about 6 and a half minutes. In a separate bowl, add the eggs and beat, then stir in the 1 3/4 cups of ricotta cheese, 1/2 cup of freshly grated Romano cheese, 1 teaspoon of onion powder, 1 teaspoon of garlic powder and the 1/2 teaspoon of salt. Add the spinach / carrots / onions to the cheese mixture and stir to combine.

Preheat the oven to 350 degrees Fahrenheit. Build the lasagna while the oven is heating by first ladeling some of the tomato sauce in the bottom. Next layer half of the eggplant noodles, then spoon half of the cheese mixture over the noodles, then half of the tomato sauce mixture. Repeat the layers and top by sprinkling the cup of shredded mozzarella cheese. Cover and bake for 35 minutes, then remove the cover and bake the last 10 minutes. Allow to sit for at least 10 minutes, to help the sauces set and cool before serving.

Pork Roast and Stuffing

This is not the kind of stuffing you may be thinking about, it is delicious stuffed mushrooms with not a grain in sight.

Makes 6 servings.

Ingredients:

*1 pork (or lamb) roast (boneless - at least 2 pounds)
*16 bacon slices (divided 6 and 10)
*12 mushrooms (large caps only)
*1 1/2 cups of spicy mustard (divided in half)
*1/4 cup of onion (minced)
*2 mushrooms (large, chopped)

Directions:

Prep: Preheat oven to 350 degrees Fahrenheit.

Poke a fork over the surface of the pork roast. Place the roast in a roasting pan. Brush most of the 3/4 cup of spicy mustard over the poked holes and surface. Take 10 strips of bacon and wrap over the top, aiming to cover the roast. Brush the bacon with a little of the spicy mustard. Bake for an hour, making sure the pork is well done (145 degrees Fahrenheit in the center). Cook the remaining 6 slices of bacon to crispy. Crumble the bacon and mix with the 3/4 cup of spicy mustard, 1/4 cup of minced onion and the 2 chopped mushrooms. Place the mushroom caps upside down in a baking dish. Divide the bacon mixture among the 12 caps. Place in the oven and bake for half an hour. When done, place the pork roast on a serving platter, place the 12 stuffed mushroom caps around the pork roast, and serve.

Boneless Buffalo Chicken

A delicious treat or part of the main meal, these boneless buffalo chicken nuggets are going to have them asking for seconds.

Makes 8 servings.

Ingredients:

*3 chicken breasts
*canola oil for frying
*5 tablespoons of hot pepper sauce
*4 tablespoons of butter
*1 tablespoon of vinegar (white distilled)
*salt and pepper to season

Directions:

Pour enough oil in a heavy frying pan to fry the chicken and turn the heat to medium high. Cut the 3 chicken breasts into 8 "nuggets", for a total of 24. Add the chicken to the hot oil and "fry" until they are no longer pink in the middle, about 10 minutes. Place the fried chicken on paper towels to drain the oil. In another skillet place the 4 tablespoons of butter and add the 5 tablespoons of hot pepper sauce and tablespoon of white distilled vinegar when the butter is melted. Stir and add salt and pepper to season. Add the 24 chicken nuggets to the sauce and turn the heat to low. Stir until all pieces are well coated in the sauce. Simmer for a few minutes and serve hot.

Chili Chicken Breasts

This spicy chicken breast is sure to be a hit for those who love an explosion of flavor.

Makes 8 servings.

Ingredients:

*8 chicken breast halves (beat down to quarter of an inch thick)
*1 cup of cheddar cheese (shredded)
*1/2 cup of green bell pepper (chopped)
*1/2 cup of red bell pepper (chopped)
*1/2 cup of cilantro (minced)
*1/2 cup of tomatoes (diced)
*1 teaspoon of chili powder
*1 teaspoon of cumin (ground)
*1/4 teaspoon of salt

Directions:

Preheat oven to 300 degrees Fahrenheit.

Add the cup of shredded cheddar cheese along with the 1/2 cups of chopped green bell peppers, red bell peppers, minced cilantro, and diced tomatoes. Toss in the teaspoons of chili powder and ground cumin. Sprinkle the 1/4 teaspoon of salt. Take the thin chicken breasts and press into the mixture, coating both sides.

Carefully roll the breasts, sticking a toothpick in to secure. Put each of the chicken breasts in a baking dish; sprinkle the remainder of the cheese and vegetable mixture over the top. Seal with foil and place in oven for 2 to 3 hours. Check the chicken; it is done when the chicken is no longer pink. (If using a meat thermometer - internal temperature should be 160 degrees Fahrenheit.)

Side Dishes

Squash Cakes

Squash cakes makes for a nice vegetable side dish.

Makes 8 servings.

Ingredients:

*4 cups of butternut squash (grated)
*1/2 cup of onion (diced)
*1/2 cup of garbanzo-fava bean flour
*1/2 cup of sour cream
*2 eggs
*6 tablespoons of olive oil
*6 tablespoons of corn flour
*4 tablespoons pumpkin seeds
*2 tablespoons of olive oil
*2 teaspoons of curry powder
*1 teaspoon of cumin (ground)
*1 teaspoon of salt
*1 teaspoon of pepper (ground black)

Directions:

Put a skillet on medium heat and pour the 2 tablespoons of olive oil. Add the 1/2 cup of diced onion and sauté.

Add the 4 cups of butternut. Sprinkle the 2 teaspoons of curry powder, teaspoons of ground cumin, salt and black pepper. Toss to distribute the seasonings evenly. Beat 2 eggs in a cup, then pour over the squash and add the 1/2 cup of garbanzo-fava bean flour and the 6 tablespoons of corn flour. Stir in the sautéed onions. Add 4 tablespoons of olive oil to the skillet and turn to medium heat. Add about a fourth cup of the butternut squash shreds and using a spatula flatten to a patty, about a quarter of an inch thick. Fry for a few minutes until crisp, flip and repeat. Do this until all of the squash is fried, about 8 servings worth. Add a dollop of sour cream and sprinkle some pumpkin seeds on top.

Spicy Turkey Stuffing

You can have your bird and stuffing too! This is a spicy stuffing made with rice instead of bread and makes enough to feed a large crowd.

Makes 20 servings.

Ingredients:

*5 cartons of chicken stock (32 oz cartons)
*10 cups of rice (uncooked white)
*1 pound of sausage (pork - bulk)
*1 pound of ground beef
*1 1/2 cups of celery (chopped)
*1 1/2 cups of onion (chopped and divided into 1 cup and 1/2 cup)
*1 tablespoon of garlic (minced)
*1 tablespoon of thyme (dried)
*1 tablespoon of parsley (dried)
*1 tablespoon of oregano (dried)

Directions:

Add the 5 cartons of chicken stock to a large pot, stir in the 10 cups of uncooked white rice, 1 1/2 cups of chopped celery, 1 cup of chopped onion, and turn heat to high. Bring liquid to a boil, turn to low, place a lid on the pot, and simmer for about 25 minutes, until the rice is tender. While the rice is cooking, add the pound of bulk pork sausage, ground beef in a skillet, and cook on medium high heat. Add 1/2 cup of onion and the tablespoon of minced garlic and brown the meat. Drain off the fat and add the cooked meat into the pot of rice. Stir in the tablespoons of dried thyme, dried parsley, and dried oregano. The "stuffing" is ready - to stuff inside the turkey. Alternatively, it can be served alongside the turkey or chicken.

Gravy

This is a basic gravy recipe, and it will take on the flavor of whatever meat drippings you use. It goes well over meat, potatoes, or as a dipping sauce for chicken nuggets.

Makes a little over a cup.

Ingredients:

*meat drippings (enough to cover the bottom of the skillet)
*1 cup of water (or milk if you perfer a milk based gravy)
*1 or 2 teaspoons of potato flour (heaping)
*salt and pepper to season
Heat the meat drippings and sprinkle in the potato flour, stirring until it becomes a grainy paste. Add more potato flour if needed. Slowly add the cup of water (or milk) and turn the heat to medium high. Stirring often until the gravy is well blended and thickened. Season with salt and pepper.
This is the type of recipe you will have to eyeball it and add or take away ingredients as needed. Different meat drippings will react with the consistency, so play with the amounts until it turns out like you want.

Creamy Mushroom Soup

This hearty soup makes for a nice hot lunch or as part of the supper.

Makes 8 to 10 servings.

Ingredients:

*8 cups of chicken stock
*1 pound of mushrooms (chopped shitake)
*3/4 cup of onions (chopped)
*2 tablespoons of olive oil
*1/2 teaspoon of salt
*black ground pepper to season

Directions:

Pour the 2 tablespoons of olive oil in a large soup pot. Turn heat to medium. Stir in the 3/4 cup of chopped onions for about 20 minutes, stirring often. Add the pound of chopped shitake mushrooms and continue sautéing for another 7 minutes. Pour the 8 cups of chicken stock, turning heat to high and bring to boil. Reduce heat to low and simmer for another ten minutes. Pour soup into a blender and blend for a couple of minutes. Serve hot.

Chicken Stuffing

If you love having stuffing with your chicken, you can again with this gluten free stuffing.

Makes 8 servings.

Ingredients:

*2 cups of chicken stock
*2 cups of rice (instant white)
*1 tablespoon of onion (dried minced)
*1 tablespoon of butter
*2 teaspoons of celery (dried flakes)
*1 teaspoon of parsley (dried)
*1/4 teaspoon of salt
*1/8 teaspoon of sage (dried)
*1/8 teaspoon of thyme (dried)

Directions:

In a saucepan add the 2 cups of chicken stock, tablespoon of dried minced onion, tablespoon of butter, 2 teaspoons of dried celery flakes, teaspoon of dried parsley flakes, 1/4 teaspoon of salt, 1/8 teaspoon of dried sage, and 1/8 teaspoon of dried thyme. Turn heat to high and bring to a rolling boil. Add the 2 cups of instant white rice and turn the heat off. Allow to sit until the rice absorbs the liquid and tenderizes, about 7 minutes. Serve as stuffing with chicken.

Breads

Cheese Bread

This bread makes a perfect companion for Italian dishes.

Makes 6 servings.

Ingredients:

*2 cups of tapioca flour
*2/3 cup of Parmesan cheese (grated)
*1/2 cup of olive oil
*1/3 cup of water
*1/3 cup of milk
*2 eggs
*2 teaspoons of garlic (minced)
*1 teaspoon of salt

Directions:

Prep: Preheat the oven to 375 degrees Fahrenheit.

Add the 1/2 cup of olive oil to the 1/3 cup of water and teaspoon of salt to a saucepan. Turn the heat to high and bring to a boil. Immediately remove the pan from the heat and quickly stir in the 2 cups of tapioca flour and the 2 teaspoons of mince garlic. Stir to combine and leave for about 12 minutes. Next stir in the 2/3 cup of grated Parmesan cheese. Beat the 2 eggs and stir them into the batter. Batter will be lumpy. Divide into 6 lumps and place on a baking sheet. (do not grease the sheet) Bake for about 17 minutes until the tops of the "lumps" turn a golden brown.

Flax Bread

This bread makes a great side dish with a nice supper. It goes well with soups and stews.

Makes 1 small loaf.

Ingredients:

*1/2 cup of coconut flour
*1/2 cup of flax seeds (ground)
*1/4 cup of coconut oil (melted)
*1/8 cup of water
*5 eggs
*1 teaspoon of baking soda
*1 teaspoon of lemon juice
*1/2 teaspoon of salt

Prep: Preheat oven to 325 degrees Fahrenheit. Spray a 7.75x4.5x3 inch loaf pan with cooking spray.

Mix together the 1/2 cup of coconut flour, 1/2 cup of ground flax seeds, 1 teaspoon of baking soda and 1/2 teaspoon of salt. In a separate bowl, add the 1/4 cup of melted coconut oil and stir in the 1/8 cup of water. Beat the 5 eggs and add to the liquid along with the teaspoon of lemon juice.

Gradually add the dry ingredients into the wet and beat with an electric beater for a couple of minutes, the batter will be thick. Put the dough in the loaf pan and bake until inserted toothpick in the center comes out clean and the top is golden brown, about 40 minutes.

Pumpkin Bread

If you want to make the house smell good, bake some pumpkin bread, then eat it for dessert.

Makes 1 loaf.

Ingredients:

*1 cup of almond flour
*1/2 cup of coconut oil (melted)
*1/2 cup of pumpkin (pureed)
*1/4 cup of coconut flour
*1/8 cup of pumpkin seeds
*4 eggs
*3 tablespoons of pumpkin pie spice
*2 tablespoons of honey
*2 tablespoons of sugar (granulated)
*1/2 teaspoon of baking powder
*1/2 teaspoon of salt
*1/2 teaspoon of cinnamon (ground)

Directions:

Prep: Preheat the oven to 350 degrees Fahrenheit. Spray a regular sized loaf pan with cooking spray.

Mix the dry ingredients together, 1 cup of almond flour, 1/4 cup of coconut flour, 3 tablespoons of pumpkin pie spice, 1/2 teaspoon of baking powder, 1/2 teaspoon of salt, and 1/2 teaspoon of ground cinnamon in a bowl. In a separate bowl add the eggs and beat. Mix in the 1/2 cup of melted coconut oil, 1/2 cup of pureed pumpkin, 2 tablespoons of honey, and the 2 tablespoons of granulated sugar. Stir in the flour ingredients, mixing well. Pour the batter into the loaf pan. Spread the 1/8 cup of pumpkin seeds over the top of the batter. Bake until an inserted toothpick in the center comes out clean, start checking at half an hour (it may take an extra 15 minutes or more, depending on the oven). Allow pumpkin bread to completely cool before taking out of the loaf pan.

Sweet Pan Bread

A delicious white cake that you can top with your favorite cake topping.

Makes a 13x9 single layer.

Ingredients:

*3 cups of rice flour (white)
*2 cups of buttermilk
*1 cup of tapioca flour
*1 cup of sugar (granulated)
*2 eggs
*2 teaspoons of baking soda
*2 teaspoons of baking powder
*2 teaspoons of salt

Directions:

Prep: Preheat oven to 350 degrees Fahrenheit. Spray a 13x9 inch pan with cooking spray.

In a bowl, add the 3 cups of white rice flour, 1 cup of tapioca flour, 1 cup of granulated sugar, 2 teaspoons of baking soda, 2 teaspoons of baking powder, and 2 teaspoons of salt and mix. In a separate bowl, crack the 2 eggs and beat well. Stir in the 2 cups of buttermilk. Pour the liquid into the center of the flour mixture, stir gently, not over-stirring. Pour the batter into the prepared 13x9 pan. Bake until an inserted toothpick in the center comes out clean and the surface is golden brown, a little over an hour. Cool for about 10 minutes before serving. Store in a sealed container at room temperature.

Bread Rolls

Grain free rolls are delicious served with breakfast or a warm and tasty side with a full meal. Or enjoy a roll with butter and jam as a snack.

Makes a dozen rolls.

Ingredients:

*2 cups of arrowroot (heaping)
*1 1/2 cups of water
*1cup of quinoa flour
*1/4 cup of canola oil
*2 eggs
*2 teaspoons of cream of tartar
*1 teaspoon of baking soda
*1 teaspoon of salt
Prep: Preheat oven to 350 degrees Fahrenheit. Spray a large baking sheet with cooking spray or use a sheet of baking paper.
Mix the 2 heaping cups of arrowroot with the 1 cup of quinoa flour, 2 teaspoons of cream of tartar, 1 teaspoon of baking soda and 1 teaspoon of salt. Add the 2 eggs, 1/4 cup of canola oil and 1 1/2 cups of water, blending well. Divide and dollop by spoon 12 "rolls" onto the

baking sheet. If there is not enough room, use 2 baking sheets. Bake until tops are a golden brown, half an hour.

Pizza Crust

A delicious pizza crust you can top in any way you see fit to make a delicious pizza.

Makes two large pizzas.

Ingredients:

*2 1/8 cups of water (warm)
*1 cup of quinoa flour
*1 cup of buckwheat
*1/4 cup of potato flour
*1/4 cup of arrowroot
*2 tablespoons of canola oil
*4 teaspoons of yeast (dry)
*2 teaspoons of salt
*2 teaspoons of sugar (granulated)
*2 teaspoons of guar gum

Directions:

Prep: Spray 2 large pizza pans with cooking spray.

Mix the cup of quinoa flour with the cup of buckwheat, 1/4 cup of potato flour, 1/4 cup of arrowroot, 2 teaspoons of salt, 2 teaspoons of granulated sugar and 2 teaspoons of guar gum in a bowl. Add in the 4 teaspoons of dry yeast, mixing thoroughly. Mix the 2 1/8 cups of warm water with the 2 tablespoons of canola oil. Slowly add the liquid to the flour mix, using a wooden spoon to stir. Stir well to mix thoroughly until the dough becomes sticky. If the dough is too dry after adding all the liquid, add a touch of warm water. You want the dough a sticky consistency, sticking to the spoon when held upside down. Next, using a spatula spread about a third of the the sticky dough onto the prepared pizza pan. The dough will stretch thin, but will rise thicker.

Allow pizza crusts to rise while preheating the oven to 350 degrees Fahrenheit, about 20 minutes. Bake in preheated oven for 20 minutes. Remove and top with your favorite pizza toppings and return to hot oven for another 10 minutes.

Rye Bread

Here's a tasty bread for rye lovers.

Makes 6 to 8 servings.

Ingredients:

*2 cups of almond flour (blanched)
*1 1/2 cups of flaxmeal (golden)
*1/2 cup of water
*6 eggs
*4 tablespoons of olive oil
*3 tablespoons of caraway seeds
*2 teaspoons of agave nectar
*1 1/2 teaspoon of cream of tartar
*1 teaspoon of salt
*1 teaspoon of baking soda

Directions:

Prep: Preheat oven to 350 degrees Fahrenheit. Grease a 9x5 loaf pan with cooking spray.

Mix the 2 cups of blanched almond flour with the 1 1/2 cups of golden flaxmeal, 1 1/2 teaspoons of cream of tartar, teaspoon of salt, and teaspoon of baking soda. In a separate bowl, combine the 1/2 cup of water with the 6 eggs using a whisk then add 4 tablespoons of olive oil and the 3 tablespoons of agave nectar. Gently fold the batter into the flour mix. Stir in the 3 tablespoons of caraway seeds. Set to the side for 2 minutes. Spoon the batter/dough into the greased loaf pan. Bake until the top is crusty brown, about 35 minutes. Allow to cool before serving.

Walnutty Crackers

Walnutty crackers make a good replacement for saltines.

Makes 96 crackers.

Ingredients:

*3 cups of almond flour (blanched)
*1 cup of walnuts (finely chopped)
*2 eggs
*2 tablespoons of olive oil
*1 1/2 teaspoons of salt

Directions:

Prep: Preheat oven to 350 degrees Fahrenheit. Combine the 3 cups of blanched almond flour with the cup of finely chopped walnuts, 2 eggs, 2 tablespoons of olive oil and 1 1/2 teaspoon of salt. Use your hands to mix well, separate into two dough balls. Put parchment paper over 2 16x12 inch baking sheets. Add a dough ball to the center of each, then place another sheet of parchment paper over the dough and roll out until it covers the bottom of the baking sheet. Do so with both and discard the top sheets. Next, use a pizza cutter and cut 6 lines lengthwise and 8 widthwise making 48 "crackers" on each pan. Bake the crackers until the tops turn a golden brown, about 11 minutes. Cool completely before serving.

Desserts and Snacks

Mini Cheesecakes

Cheesecakes are always a delightful and decadent dessert.

Makes a dozen and a half cheesecakes.

Ingredients:

*3 packages of cream cheese (8 oz packages - room temperature)
*1 cup of sour cream
*2 cups of sugar (granulated - divided)
*5 eggs
*2 teaspoons of vanilla extract (divided)

Directions:

Prep: Preheat the oven to 350 degrees Fahrenheit. Place cupcake liners in 18 cupcake pan cups.

Using an electric mixer beat the cream cheese with 1 cup of granulated sugar. Add the 5 eggs, one at a time, running the beaters. Last, add 1 teaspoon of vanilla extract, beat for 30 seconds more. Spoon the batter evenly in the 18 lined cupcake cups. Bake in the oven until the tops turn golden brown for half an hour. Cool for at least 10 minutes. Put the cup of sour cream in a bowl along with the cup of sugar and teaspoon of vanilla extract and using a whisk blend the ingredients. Place a dollop of sour cream topping on top of each cheesecake. Place back in the hot oven for another 6 minutes. Place cupcake tin on a wire rack for cooling. Wait until they are completely cool before removing from the tin.

Banana Nut Brownies

Extra moist chocolate brownies with the fresh flavor of bananas.

Makes 20 servings.

Ingredients:

*2 bananas (ripe)
*2 cups of sugar (granulated)
*1 1/2 cups of canola oil
*1 cup of potato flour
*1 cup of rice flour (brown)
*1/2 cup of cocoa powder (unsweetened)
*1 1/2 teaspoon of salt
*3/4 teaspoon of cream of tartar
*1/2 teaspoon of baking soda

Directions:

Prep: Preheat the oven to 325 degrees Fahrenheit. Spray a 13x9 inch baking pan with cooking spray.

Mix the 2 cups of granulated sugar with the 1 cup of potato flour, 1 cup of brown rice flour, 1/2 cup of unsweetened cocoa powder, 1 1/2 teaspoon of salt, 3/4 teaspoon of cream of tartar and the 1/2 teaspoon of baking soda. Set aside and in a separate bowl mash the 2 ripe bananas and stir in the 1 1/2 cups of canola oil.

Add the dry ingredients and blend well. Spoon the batter into the prepared 13x9 inch baking pan. Bake until the top is dry to the touch, about 23 or more minutes. Cool and cut into 20 squares.

Spicy Almond Pudding

For the pudding lovers there is an answer to grain-free pudding, this recipe gives a delicious and spicy pudding that is good hot or cold.

Makes 8 servings.

Ingredients:

*4 cups of milk
*2 cups of almond flour
*3/4 cups of sugar (granulated)
*1 teaspoon of cinnamon (ground)
*1 teaspoon of espresso powder (instant)
*1 teaspoon of vanilla extract
*1/2 teaspoon of cardamom (ground)

Directions:

Add the 4 cups of milk, 2 cups of almond flour, 3/4 cup of granulated sugar, teaspoon of instant espresso powder and 1/2 teaspoon of ground cardamom. Stir over medium heat before it boils, turn heat to low and continue stirring often for about 20 minutes. Pudding will thicken. Pour pudding in a serving bowl and stir in the teaspoon of vanilla extract. Chill overnight for best results, or at least for several hours.

Brownies

Everyone who loves chocolate will not turn down a plate of these warm brownies.

Makes 8 small servings.

Ingredients:

*1/2 cup of honey
*1/2 cup of carob powder
*1/2 cup of pecan meal
*1/4 cup of arrowroot
*2 eggs
*6 tablespoons of canola oil

Directions:

Prep: Preheat oven to 350 degrees Fahrenheit. Spray an 8x8 baking pan with cooking spray.

Combine the 1/2 cups of carob powder, pecan meal with the 1/4 cup of arrowroot. In a separate bowl, beat the 2 eggs then mix in the 1/2 cup of honey and the 6 tablespoons of canola oil. Stir in the dry ingredients. Pour batter into prepared pan and bake until inserted toothpick in the center comes out clean, about 20 minutes.

Choco-Peanut Butter Tart

Yes, this is a pie that is fit for the most royal of desserts.
And grain free too.
Makes 1 9 inch tart.

First, make the chocolate pudding:
Ingredients:

*1 can of coconut milk (regular, 13.5 ounces)
*1 cup of semi-sweet chocolate chips
*5 tablespoons of agave nectar
*2 tablespoons of arrowroot
*1 tablespoon of vanilla extract
*pinch of salt

Place a saucepan on medium heat and pour the can of
coconut milk and the pinch of salt. Stir in the 2
tablespoons of arrowroot, then using a whisk, stir/beat
for about 2 minutes. Contining with the whisk, add the
5 tablespoons of arrowroot and 1 tablespoon of vanilla
extract. Turn the heat off and cool for a couple of
minutes before stirring in the cup of semi-sweet
chocolate chips. Stir until all chips are melted. Set
aside.

Make the tart crust next.

Ingredients:

*1 1/2 cups of peanuts (roasted)
*2 tablespoons of canola oil
*2 tablespoons of molasses
*1/4 teaspoon of salt
*1/4 teaspoon of baking soda

Directions:

Prep: Preheat oven to 350 degrees Fahrenheit. Lightly spray a 9 inch tart pan.

Pour the 1 1/2 cups of roasted peanuts into a food processor and grind to a crunchy texture. Add in the 1/4 teaspoons of salt and the 1/4 teaspoon of baking soda, pulse for a few seconds. Do the same with the 2 tablespoons of canola oil and the 2 tablespoons of molasses. Pulse until it forms a dough. Press the tart crust dough into the 9 inch tart pan. Bake in preheated oven until it turns a golden brown, about 8 minutes. Remove from oven and cool. Pour the chocolate pudding into the crust. Chill about half an hour before serving.

Apple Cranberry Cobbler

Enjoy a hot apple and cranberry cobbler with your favorite topping of ice cream or whipped cream.

Makes about 5 servings.

Ingredients:

*4 1/3 cups of sliced apples (peeled and cored)
*1 can of cranberries (16 ounce whole berries)
*1 cup of oats
*1/4 cup of applesauce (unsweetened)
*1/4 cup of soy milk
*2 tablespoons of brown sugar
*1/2 teaspoon of cinnamon (ground)

Directions:

Prep: Preheat the oven to 375 degrees Fahrenheit. Add the 4 1/3 cup of sliced apples and the can of cranberries to an 8 inch baking dish and stir. In a bowl, add the cup of oats, 2 tablespoons of brown sugar with the 1/2 teaspoon of ground cinnamon and mix. Add the 1/4 cups of unsweetened applesauce and soy milk, stirring. Using a large spoon, spoon the "crust" over the fruit, careful not to mix in with the fruit. Press the crust down on top with the back of the large spoon. Place in preheated oven for about 45 minutes, until the crust is golden and crisp. Cool before serving.

Hint: This is delicious served warm with vanilla ice cream.

Cookies

Macaroons

Macaroons are delightful cookies that are light and crispy. These are rich in coconut and vanilla.

Makes 3 dozen cookies.

Ingredients:

*3 cups of coconut (unsweetened and shredded)
*1 1/2 cups of almond flour (blanched, fine ground)
*3/4 cup of honey
*1/2 cup of coconut oil
*4 teaspoons of vanilla extract
*1/4 teaspoon of salt

Directions:

Prep: Preheat oven to 200 degrees Fahrenheit. Place parchment on a cookie sheet.

First, mix the dry ingredients of the 1 1/2 cups of find ground blanched almond flour with the 1/4 teaspoon of salt. Add the 3 cups of shredded unsweetened coconut. In a separate bowl, combine the 3/4 cup of honey with the 1/2 cup of coconut oil and the 4 teaspoons of vanilla extract. Stir in the dry ingredients. Drop the cookie dough by the tablespoonful onto a cookie sheet, evenly spacing a dozen cookies on the sheet. Bake until the outside of the cookie is dry and crisp, but the inside will be soft, about 47 minutes. Cool for at least 15 minutes before serving.

Walnut Cookies

These sweet walnut cookies are a crowd pleaser.

Makes 2 1/2 dozen cookies.

Ingredients:

*4 cups of walnuts (finely chopped)
*1/4 cup of honey
*4 egg whites
*2 tablespoons of cinnamon (ground)

Directions:

Prep: Preheat oven to 350 degrees.

Make sure the 4 cups of walnuts are finely chopped or even ground. Add the 1/4 cup of honey and toss. Put the 4 egg whites in a cup and beat with a whisk until they are frothy. Add to the walnuts and stir. Drop by the spoonfuls onto an ungreased cookie sheet, enough to make 30. Keep the cookies about 3 to a row and 4 rows on a standard cookie sheet. Bake for 15 minutes and remove.

Peanut Butter Cookies

This is a timeless classic for peanut butter lovers.

Makes 3 dozen cookies.

Ingredients:

*2 cups of peanut butter
*2 cups of sugar (granulated) (plus extra for sprinkling)
*2 eggs
*2 teaspoons of vanilla extract
*1/4 teaspoon of salt

Directions:

Prep: Preheat oven to 350 degrees Fahrenheit.

Add the 2 eggs to a bowl and beat. Next combine the 2 cups of peanut butter, 2 cups of granulated sugar, 2 teaspoons of vanilla extract, and the 1/4 teaspoon of salt with the beaten eggs. Measure about a tablespoon of cookie dough on the cookie sheet. Make criss-cross pattern with a fork, keep the cookies about an inch apart. Sprinkle a pinch of granulated sugar on the top of the unbaked cookies. Bake in heated oven for around 10 minutes or until the tops and edges turn a golden brown.

Variations: Add mini chocolate chips to make peanut

butter chocolate chip cookies. Use crunchy peanut butter for a nutty crunch.

Chocolate Nut Cookie Bars

These are much better than a candy bar any day.

Makes around 20 cookie bars.

Ingredients:

*2 cups of sugar (granulated)
*2 cups of peanut butter
*1 cup of coconut flakes
*1 can of sweetened condensed milk (14 oz)
*3/4 cup of chocolate chips (semisweet)
*3/4 cup of chocolate chips (dark)
*1/2 cup of pecans (chopped)
*1/2 cup of almonds (chopped)
*2 eggs

Directions:

Prep: Preheat oven to 350 degrees Fahrenheit. Use parchment paper and line a 13x9 inch baking dish.

Add the 2 eggs to a bowl and beat, then stir in the 2 cups of granulated sugar. Next add the 2 cups of peanut butter and blend well. Pour the batter in the baking dish and bake for just 8 minutes. This forms the bottom layer of the bars. Sprinkle the cup of coconut flakes, 3/4 cup of semisweet chocolate chips, 3/4 cup of dark chocolate chips, 1/2 cup of chopped pecans, and the 1/2 cup of

almonds over the cookie bar base.   Pour the 14 oz. can
of sweetened condensed milk evenly over the top. Bake
for another half an hour. Allow cookie bars to cool
before removing from baking dish and onto a cutting
board. Cut into 20 bars and remove the parchment
paper.

Cakes

Orange Cake

This is a delicious orange cake, super moist with a delightful citrus flavor. Make a simple sugar icing to drizzle over the top after you drizzle the orange juice if desired.

Makes a 13x9 cake.

Ingredients:

*1 cup of coconut flour
*3/4 cup of honey
*1/2 cup of coconut oil (melted and cooled)
*1/2 cup of milk
*12 eggs (warmed to room temperature)
*1 orange (juiced)
*2 teaspoons of vanilla extract
*1 teaspoon of orange zest
*1 teaspoon of baking powder
*1 teaspoon of salt

Directions:

Prep: Preheat oven to 350 degrees Fahrenheit. Spray a 13x9 inch pan with cooking spray.

Add the dozen eggs to a bowl and whisk well. Stir in the 3/4 cup of honey, 1/2 cup of coconut milk, , 2 teaspoons of vanilla extract and the teaspoon of orange zest. Next, stir in the 1/2 cup of melted and cooled coconut oil, blending well. In a separate bowl combine the cup of coconut flour, teaspoons of baking powder and salt. Gradually add the dry ingredients into the batter, blending. Pour the batter into the prepared 13x9 in pan and bake until a toothpick inserted in the center comes out clean, about 37 minutes. Cool for 5 mintues. Poke holes in the top of the cake with a small knife or fork and drizzle the juice from the orange over the top.

Almond Cake

This cake gives a full nutty flavor and completely grain free.

Makes one 9-inch round cake.

Ingredients:

*1 3/4 cups of almond flour
*1/2 cup of honey + 2 tablespoons
*1/4 cup of almonds (slivered)
*4 eggs (separated at room temperature)
*1 teaspoon of vanilla extract
*1/2 teaspoon of baking soda
*1/2 teaspoon of salt

Directions:

Prep: Preheat the oven to 350 degrees Fahrenheit. Spray a 9 inch spring form pan with cooking spray. Place parchment paper in the bottom of the pan.

Add the 4 egg yolks to a bowl with the 1/2 cup of honey and teaspoon of vanilla extract. Beat with an electric mixer until combined. In a separate bowl add the 1 3/4 cups of almond flour along with the 1/2 teaspoon of baking soda and 1/2 teaspoons of salt and blend. Gradually add the dry ingredients to the batter, using the electric mixer to blend. In another separate bowl add the 4 egg whites and beat with the electric mixer until it forms stiff peaks, about 90 seconds. Fold the egg whites into the batter using a wooden spoon. Pour the batter into the prepared spring form pan. Bake until toothpick inserted in the middle comes out clean, about half an hour. Cool in the spring form pan for 10 minutes, then turn out onto a cake platter. "Frost" with the 2 tablespoons of honey, by drizzling over the top, and garnish with the 1/4 cup of slivered almonds.

Carrot Cake

For carrot cake lovers, this cake tastes just as good as the original, moist and delicious. Frost with your favorite cream cheese frosting and you can hardly tell the difference.

Makes 1 9-inch round cake.

Ingredients:

*3 cups of almond flour
*1 1/2 cups of carrots
*1/2 cup of honey
*6 eggs (yolks and whites separate)
*1 tablespoon of orange rind (grated)
*1 tablespoon of orange juice

Directions:

Prep: Preheat oven to 325 degrees Fahrenheit. Spray a 9 inch spring form pan with cooking spray.

First, cook the carrots until tender, then puree in a blender or food processor. Next, separate the 6 eggs. Beat the egg yolks and mix in with the 1/2 cup of honey. Stir in the cooked pureed carrots along with the tablespoons of grated orange rind and orange juice. Fold in the 3 cups of almond flour. In a separate bowl, using an electric mixer, beat the 6 egg whites until stiff

peaks form. Gently fold the egg whites into the batter.
Pour batter into the prepared spring form pan. Bake
until toothpick inserted in the middle comes out clean, a
little under an hour. Allow the cake to cool in the pan
for 15 minutes before removing it to a wire rack. Frost
as desired when completely cool.

Yellow Cake

This is a basic yellow cake recipe. Frost with your favorite frosting or fruit and whipped topping.

Makes a double layer round cake or a single layer 13x9 cake.

Ingredients:

*1 1/2 cups of rice flour (white)
*1 1/4 cup of sugar (granulated)
*1 cup of milk
*2/3 cup of mayonnaise
*3/4 cup of tapioca flour
*4 eggs (slightly beaten)
*3 teaspoons of baking powder
*2 teaspoons of vanilla extract
*1 teaspoon of arrowroot
*1 teaspoon of salt
*1 teaspoon of baking soda

Directions:

Prep: Preheat oven to 350 degrees Fahrenheit. Spray either 2 9 inch cake pans or 1 13x9 inch pan with cooking spray.

In a bowl add the 1 1/2 cups of white rice flower, 3/4 cup of tapioca flour, 3 teaspoons of baking powder, the teaspoons of arrowroot, salt, and baking soda and sift together. In a separate bowl, add the 1 1/4 cup of granulated sugar, 2/3 cup of mayonnaise and the 4 slightly beaten eggs and mix well. Slowly add the flour mixture, and beat with electric beaters for a minute. Pour in the cup of milk and the 2 teaspoons of vanilla extract and beat an additional 2 minutes. Pour the batter into the prepared cake pan(s). Bake until an inserted toothpick in the middle comes out clean and top is a golden brown, about 25 minutes. Cool before frosting.

Sponge Cake

Here is a recipe for cake completely free of wheat grain and you would never know it from the taste. It is delicious to spread your favorite frosting or fresh fruit over the top.

Ingredients:

*4 eggs (yolks and whites separate)
*3/4 cup of sugar (granulated)
*3/4 cup of potato flour
*1/4 cup of arrowroot
*1 teaspoon of cream of tarter
*1/2 teaspoon of baking soda
*1/4 teaspoon of salt

Directions:

Prep: Preheat the oven to 350 degrees Fahrenheit. Spray either a 13x9 inch pan or 2 9 inch round cake pans with cooking spray. Alternatively line with baking paper sheets.

In a bowl add the 4 egg whites and beat with an electric mixer until stiff peaks form. Add the 3/4 cup of granulated sugar while running the mixer. Next, pour in the egg yolks, continue to beat until mixed. In a separate bowl, mix the 3/4 cup of potato flour, 1/4 cup of arrowroot, 1/2 teaspoon of baking soda and the 1/4 teaspoon of salt. Gradually add to the egg mixture, folding gently until all lumps are gone. Pour batter into the prepared pan(s). Bake for about 17 minutes or until the top is golden brown.

Serving suggestions: Top with fresh strawberries and whipped cream.

23734875R00117

Made in the USA
Lexington, KY
21 June 2013